THE FIRST
WORLD WAR

NIGEL KELLY

Head of History, Sacred Heart Comprehensive School,
Newcastle-upon-Tyne and a GCSE Chief Examiner

HEINEMANN
EDUCATIONAL

Heinemann Educational,
a division of Heinemann Educational Books Ltd,
Halley Court, Jordan Hill, Oxford OX2 8EJ

OXFORD LONDON EDINBURGH
MADRID ATHENS BOLOGNA PARIS
MELBOURNE SYDNEY AUCKLAND SINGAPORE TOKYO
IBADAN NAIROBI HARARE GABORONE
PORTSMOUTH NH (USA)

First published 1989

95 96 13 12 11 10 9 8

British Library Cataloguing in Publication Data

Kelly, Nigel, *1954–*
  The First World War.
  1. World War 1
  I. Title
  940.3

ISBN 0 435 31043 7

Designed and produced by
The Pen & Ink Book Company Ltd, Huntingdon

Printed and bound in Malta by Interprint Limited

Acknowledgements

The author and publisher would like to thank the following for
permission to reproduce photographs on the pages indicated:

Australian War Memorial: pp. 12 (right), 13 (top right) and 27;
British Library: pp. 60 (lower right) and 62; Culver Pictures:
p. 46 (top); Mary Evans Picture Library: p. 44; John Frost
Collection: p. 34 (lower left); Hulton-Deutsch Picture Library:
pp. 15, 23, 37 (top left), 43 and 47; Robert Hunt Library: pp. 7, 9,
20, 37 (lower right), 42 (right) and 60 (top right); Imperial War
Museum: pp. 6 (lower), 10 (lower), 12 (left), 13 (top and lower
left), 14, 16 (left), 17, 18, 22, 24, 28, 29 (lower), 36, 37 (top right
and lower left), 39 (right), 42 (left), 50, 51, 52, 53, 54, 56 (top
right) and 59; Mansell Collection: p. 34 (top); Peter Newark's
Pictures: pp. 33 (lower), 38 and 56 (lower left); *New York Times*
p. 46 (lower); Popperfoto: pp. 6 (top), 10 (top), 39 (left), 55 and
57 (top right); *Punch* Publications: p. 49; Royal Army Museum,
Brussels: p. 57 (bottom right); Solo Syndication and Literacy
Agency: p. 34 (lower right); Suddeutscher Verlag Bilderdienst:
p. 58; Topham: pp. 30 (top), 40, 41, 45 and 60 (lower left); *The
Times*: p. 16 (right); Ullstein Bilderdienst: p. 11.

Special thanks are due to Paul Kemp of the Department of
Photographs at the Imperial War Museum for his help and
advice.

The author and publisher would also like to thank George
Sassoon for permission to reproduce 'Does it matter?' by
Siegfried Sassoon, p. 53; Chappell Music Ltd and International
Music Publications for permission to reproduce the song 'Over
There' on p. 47, © 1917 Leo Keist Inc. USA.

The publishers would be pleased to hear from the copyright
holders of the following photographs and illustrations, whom they
have regretfully been unable to trace: pp. 4, 8, 29, 30 (lower) and 33
(top).

Details of Written Sources

In some sources the wording or sentence structure has been
simplified to make sure that the source is accessible.

Mark Arnold-Forster, *The World at War*, Thames-Methuen, 1981:
2.7G
J. Brooman, *The Great War*, Longman, 1985: 2.6B, 3.8F
Malcolm Brown, *Tommy Goes to War*, J. M. Dent, 1978: 2.2E, 3.2A,
4.3C, 4.4B, 4.5D and E, 5.3F and H
S. L. Case, *The First World War*, Evans Brothers, 1976: 2.4D
B. Catchpole, *A Map History of the Modern World*, Heinemann
Educational, 1968: 5.2D
Jene Clemens King (Ed.), *The First World War – Selected Documents*,
Macmillan, 1972: 2.3F
G. Coppard, *With a Machine Gun to Cambrai*, Imperial War
Museum/Jane's, 1969: 2.4E
Neil De Marco, *Looking at Evidence*, Unwin Hyman, 1988: 3.2D
J. Hamer, *The Twentieth Century*, Macmillan, 1980: 3.4B
M. Holden, *War in the Trenches*, Wayland Publishers, 1973: 5.2E
Tony Howarth, *The Great War – The Home Front*, Longman, 1976:
3.8E
R. Huggett, *Growing up in the First World War*, Batsford, 1985: 3.6C,
3.8C, 4.5H, 5.1E
A. Jamieson, *Twentieth Century World History – War and Peace
1900–45*, Edward Arnold, 1979: 5.3A
T. H. Johnson, *Oxford Companion to American History*, Oxford
University Press, 1966: 4.2F
N. Jones, *The War Walk*, Hale, 1983: 2.4C
B. H. Liddell Hart, *History of the First World War*, Cassell, 1970: 2.7C
John Ray, *The First World War*, History Broadsheets, Heinemann
Educational, 1975: 2.5C, 2.6D, 3.2B, 3.4G, 3.5B, 4.3A
Fiona Reynoldson, *The First World War – 1914–1918*, Heinemann
Educational, 1988: 1.3C, 2.8A, 3.6B, 3.8B
C. Simpson, *Lusitania*, Longman, 1972: 3.4C
L. Snellgrove, *The Modern World Since 1870*, Longman, 1968: 1.3B
L. Snellgrove, *Suffragettes and Votes for Women*, Longman, 1964:
3.7G
J. and G. Stokes, *Europe and the Modern World Since 1870*, Longman,
1973: 4.2G
A. J. P. Taylor, *History of the Twentieth Century*, New Caxton Library
Service, 1979: 2.7F, 3.1B, D and G, 3.7E, 4.2B, 5.2C
John Terraine, *White Heat: The New Warfare, 1914–18*, Sidgwick and
Jackson, 1982: 2.8B and C, 3.3A and B, 4.1E, 4.4C, E, G and H
J. Williams, *The Home Fronts*, Constable, 1972: 3.8H
Dennis Winter, *Death's Men: Soldiers of the Great War*, Allen Lane,
1978: 2.4G
Peter Young (Ed.), *Marshall Cavendish Illustrated Encyclopaedia of
World War One*, Marshall Cavendish, 1984: 3.2C, 4.2A, 4.3B

CONTENTS

1.1 THE WORLD IN 1914

The world in 1914 was very different to the world we know today. The world's **population** was only half of today's and there was much less **contact** between the people of different nations. During the twentieth century there have been a series of **inventions** which have made major changes to our way of life. Television has allowed us to learn about other people and how they live; and the development of air travel has meant that millions go abroad every year. A citizen of Britain in 1914 would have been astonished to think that people would soon travel to the other side of the world in less than a day.

There have also been major changes in the way that countries are **governed**. Today most countries govern themselves; but in 1914 many of the people of the world lived in **colonies**, ruled by a European country. As the map shows, Britain, France and Germany controlled huge areas across the globe. Control of these colonies helped the European nations grow strong. A country with an overseas empire had a cheap source of **raw materials** and a market for **home-produced goods**.

Some of these colonies were especially useful to the ruling nation because they provided **military and trading bases** in important parts of the world. Controlling Egypt, for example, enabled Britain to protect its ownership of the Suez Canal. This canal provided a short cut to India, which was one of Britain's most valuable colonies.

Today the United States and the Soviet Union are called **superpowers**. In 1914 most people would have said that **Britain** was a superpower, if the label had been used then. Britain controlled almost one-quarter of the world's land surface and more than one-quarter of its total population. British trade reached every corner of the globe, and the powerful Royal Navy dominated the seas. The United States ambassador to Britain wrote: 'I guess they really believe that the Earth belongs to them.'

Britain, however, was not the only powerful European country. By 1914 the industrial output of **Germany** had overtaken Britain's, and Germany had a large and well-equipped army. **France** too had large colonies, especially in Africa and the Far East (although the French army had been humiliated by the Germans in the Franco-Prussian War of 1870–1). Undoubtedly Europe was the world's most powerful continent. No European at the time would have believed that the situation would change so rapidly in the next few years.

Competition, however, was already emerging from the **United States**. The US population, swelled by immigration, had reached 80 million by 1900 and was more than that of Britain and France put together (see Source C). The United States was a land with vast mineral resources and huge areas of rich farmland. As the USA began to exploit these resources, it soon overtook both Germany and Britain as a producer of manufactured goods. At the beginning of the century the US government made a point of keeping out of European affairs. Yet it proved impossible to continue with this policy. When the USA came to enter the First World War in 1917, its intervention was to prove decisive.

American cartoonist's view of the new century.

A loyal Indian subject proudly displays portraits of King George V and Queen Mary.

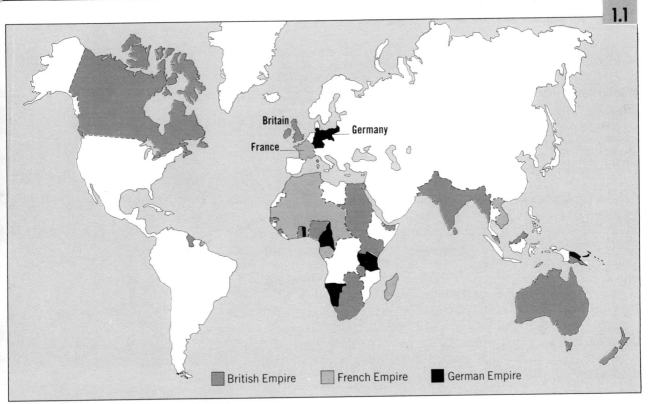

The European powers and their colonies in 1914.

| | British Empire | | French Empire | | German Empire |

SOURCE C

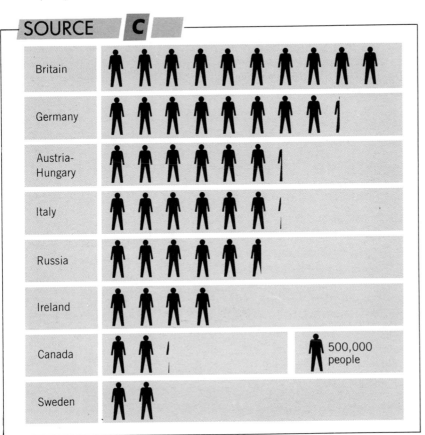

Emigration to the United States, 1830–1910 – those countries which lost a million or more citizens.

1.2 THE CAUSES OF THE WAR

Source A shows **Kaiser Wilhelm** and **King George V** talking cheerfully while on parade in London in 1911, but it fails to tell the whole story. The royal families of Britain and Germany were on good terms (Wilhelm and George were cousins), but their countries were growing further apart. Rivalry between Britain and Germany was to be a major factor in causing war in 1914.

Naval rivalry   Britain needed a strong **navy** to protect its long coastline, large Empire and valuable trade routes. For most of the nineteenth century, its navy had been larger then any two navies put together. But in 1898 when the Kaiser announced that he intended to develop the German navy, there was alarm in Britain.

But it would take the Germans years of constant shipbuilding to catch up; and Britain's lead further increased in 1906 when it launched the first of the new **Dreadnought battleships**. These were thicker-armoured, quicker and had heavier guns than any previous battleships. Yet by building these ships the British had opened the door to the Kaiser. The Dreadnoughts were so superior that they made most of the other battleships worthless. If Germany could match Britain in the launching of these new battleships, then the German navy would be able to compete on near-equal terms. In the years before the war there developed a 'naval race' as both sides tried to outbuild the other.

Colonial rivalry   The Kaiser envied Britain and France their huge **empires**. He believed that the time had come for Germany to have its 'place in the sun'. This worried Britain, because any gains Germany made could well be at Britain's expense. By the beginning of the twentieth century, Germany's highly trained and efficient army was the match of any in Europe. The Kaiser had already given the Boers of South Africa his support against the British in the war of 1899–1902 and talked about building a great German navy. Now he threatened the Empire.

Economic rivalry   Britain was the first nation to go through the Industrial Revolution. In the 1800s Britain had become rich through the manufacture and sale of home-produced goods. By 1914, however, Germany was producing more iron, more steel, more coal and even more cars. Britain's economic lead was gone.

The alliances   As Germany became a threat, Britain began to look for support against the ambitious policies of the Kaiser. For many years it had kept out of European affairs and concentrated on using the Royal Navy to protect the huge Empire. Britain had not needed alliances in Europe, especially since it might have to fight to help one of its allies. It preferred to follow the policy known as **'splendid isolation'**.

By 1900 there were two separate European alliances. Austria-Hungary, Germany and Italy were in the **Triple Alliance**. (Austria-Hungary had once controlled much of central Europe but was now less powerful and would be broken up into separate countries in 1919.) The French also felt threatened by Germany. France had suffered an overwhelming defeat by the Germans in 1871 and lost two valuable provinces, Alsace and Lorraine. Since

SOURCE **A**

Kaiser Wilhelm and George V.

SOURCE **B**

	Britain	Germany
1906	1	–
1907	3	–
1908	2	4
1909	2	3
1910	3	1
1911	5	3
1912	3	2
1913	7	3
1914	3	1
Total	29	17

Dreadnought battleships built between 1906 and 1914.

SOURCE **C**

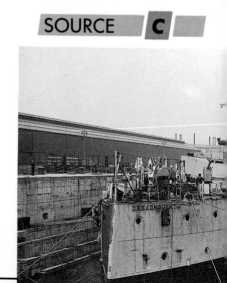

L'INGORDO
TROP DUR

An Italian cartoon showing the Kaiser's greed for an empire.

HMS 'Dreadnought', the first of the new battleships. ▼

The Balkans in 1914.

then they had been searching for allies to help fight a war of revenge. In 1894 French isolation ended when they formed an alliance with Russia.

In 1904 Britain and France signed the **Entente Cordiale** ('friendly understanding'). Three years later when Britain reached agreement with Russia the **Triple Entente** was formed. The Entente powers agreed to do no more than be on good terms, but seven years later they were allied in war against Germany and Austria-Hungary.

Although Britain did not intend to help France attack Germany, the Kaiser made several attempts to break up the agreement. In 1906 and 1911 he challenged French control of Morocco, thinking that Britain would not stand by its new friend. He was wrong. The two incidents drew the countries closer together and convinced Britain that Germany wanted war. In 1912 when they agreed that Britain would patrol the North Sea and France would guard the Mediterranean, the British and French turned their 'friendly agreement' into a **military alliance**.

Austria versus Russia   In the area of south-east Europe known as the **Balkans**, there was fierce rivalry between Austria and Russia. Here Turkey was struggling to keep its empire, while Russia and Austria clashed over who should control any area that broke free.

One such area was **Serbia**. As a Slav country it wanted to unite all the Slav people under Serbian leadership. Austria-Hungary feared that the large numbers of Slavs in its lands would want to join Serbia and so did all it could to stop the Serbians. But Russia supported Serbia. It feared that the Austrians might gain control of Constantinople and block Russia's route to the Mediterranean. A more powerful Serbia would hold Austria back.

By 1914 there was so much mistrust between members of the two alliances that it seemed only a matter of time before they went to war. The spark that finally ignited the war was to be lit in the small Bosnian town of **Sarajevo**.

1.3 WAS PRINCIP TO BLAME?

CAUSATION

On 28 June 1914 **Archduke Franz Ferdinand**, heir to the Austrian throne, went to inspect troops in the Bosnian capital of **Sarajevo**. He had been warned that his visit was dangerous, because Sarajevo was very near Austria's rival state, Serbia. Many Serbs wanted Bosnia to leave the Austrian Empire and join Serbia. Some of them were prepared to go to great lengths to show their disapproval of the Austrians.

One such Serb was **Gavrilo Princip**, a young student. He waited nervously in the streets of Sarajevo for the Archduke to arrive and then shot both Franz Ferdinand and his wife, Countess Sophie. The Austrians were furious and blamed the Serbs for helping Princip. They issued a series of demands, which Serbia accepted apart from one section. The Austrians, however, said this was not enough and declared war. Shortly afterwards the other European powers became involved, and Europe was at war.

Had Princip really caused all this?

SOURCE A

A 1914 drawing showing Princip shooting the Archduke.

SOURCE B

'As the car reversed towards him, he stepped forward and fired two shots. The first struck the Archduke's throat. The second hit Sophia in the stomach. Franz Ferdinand, blood pouring from his mouth, saw that his wife was hit. "Sophie, Sophie!" he cried out. "Don't die! Keep alive for our children." It was too late. His wife died even as he shouted. By the time the car reached the Governor's residence Franz Ferdinand was dead also.'

Account of the death of the Archduke by L. Snellgrove, 'The Modern World since 1870', 1968.

SOURCE C

Question: 'Why did you shoot Archduke Franz Ferdinand?'
Answer: 'Because people suffer so much. It is the Archduke's fault. I am a villager's son and I know how it is in the villages, so I wanted to take revenge and I am not sorry.'

From the transcript of Princip's trial, 1914.

CAUSATION

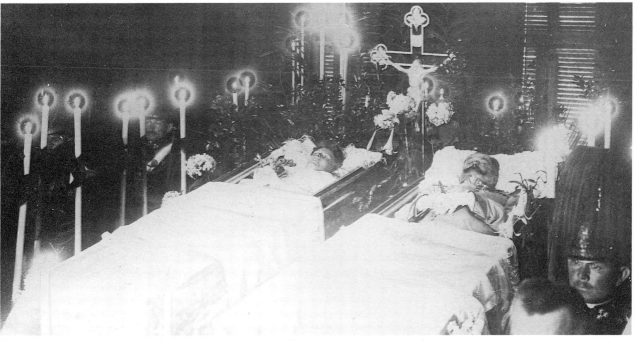

The Archduke and Countess lying in state after their assassination.

Timetable of events leading to war in 1914

28 June	Archduke assassinated
6 July	Germany promises help for Austria
23 July	Austrian ultimatum to Serbia
26 July	Russia promises help for Serbia
28 July	Austria declares war on Serbia
29 July	Germany warns Russia not to intervene
31 July	Germany warns France not to intervene
1 August	Germany declares war on Russia
3 August	Germany declares war on France; German troops enter Belgium
4 August	Britain declares war on Germany
6 August	Austria declares war on Russia

EXERCISE

1   Unit 1.2 gives the following reasons for the outbreak of war:
naval rivalry;
colonial rivalry;
economic rivalry;
the alliances;
Austria versus Russia.
Do you think that Princip was thinking of any of these points when he decided to shoot the Archduke?

2   In Source C Princip says that he killed the Archduke because 'I know how it is in the villages'. Did Princip start a world war just to improve life for the peasants?

3   'Princip killed the Archduke. The Archduke's death led to war. Therefore Princip was responsible for the outbreak of war.' Do you agree?

4   Historians have to consider a variety of causes and decide which are the most important. This can mean dividing causes of events into long-term causes, short-term causes and triggers. Long-term causes help explain why what happened in the past led up to a series of events taking place. Short-term causes explain why the events happened when they did. Triggers are what make events happen, although they are not necessarily the cause of them. Using the information in this unit, find one example of:
a   a long-term cause of the First World War;
b   a short-term cause of the First World War;
c   a trigger for the First World War.
In each case, explain why you have chosen this example.

1.4 THE OUTBREAK OF WAR

After heavily defeating France in the **Franco-Prussian War** of 1870–1, Germany had always expected that France would want a war of revenge. Since Russia and France had signed the **Dual Alliance** of 1894, Germany expected that this war would also be fought against Russia. How did Germany expect to win a war when its troops were split between battlefronts 1,000 kilometres apart?

The answer came in 1905 from the German War Minister, Count Alfred von Schlieffen. The **Schlieffen Plan** was to work as follows:

- Because Russia was a huge and relatively inefficient country, it would be slow to get its forces ready. Because Austria planned to send large forces across the Russian border at the outbreak of war, Russia would be contained. So Germany need not concern itself with fighting in the east for the first few weeks of the war.

- France had been defeated in six weeks in 1870; the same could be done again. The French would expect an attack to take place along the border between Metz and Switzerland. They had heavily fortified this area, and their own plan involved an attack on Germany from this region. What they could not foresee was a German invasion which came from the north through Belgium. Here France's defences were weak, and Paris could soon be reached and taken. The main French forces would be surrounded, and surrender would soon follow.

- Once France was defeated, the Germans could devote their full resources to fighting the Russians.

On 3 August the Schlieffen Plan was put into operation. The German Chief of Staff, von Moltke, sent an army over a million strong into **Belgium**. At the same time the German forces on the Metz border resisted the French attacks, inflicting 300,000 casualties on the French in just two weeks.

The plan soon began to go wrong, however. Until the invasion of Belgium there was a chance that Britain might stay out of the war. Now there was none. Belgium was a neutral country and in a treaty signed in 1839 Britain had agreed to defend Belgium's neutrality. The Germans claimed that Britain was going to war over **'a scrap of paper'**. The British pointed out that Prussia (which had formed the new country of Germany in 1870) had also signed the treaty. So Germany found itself at war with Britain, which sent the **British Expeditionary Force** (**BEF**) to help France.

In Belgium the German advance was slower than expected. The allies put up fierce resistance at Liège and Antwerp. The BEF (which the Kaiser referred to as a 'contemptible little army') played its part, holding up the Germans in a battle at **Mons**. The situation was made worse for the Germans when Russia took just ten days to prepare its armies. On 19 August, Russian forces entered Germany, and Germany had to withdraw troops from the Schlieffen Plan to defend its eastern border.

Count Alfred von Schlieffen.

"BELGIUM . . . . SHALL FORM AN INDEPENDENT AND PERPETUALLY NEUTRAL STATE. IT SHALL BE BOUND TO OBSERVE SUCH NEUTRALITY TOWARDS ALL OTHER STATES."

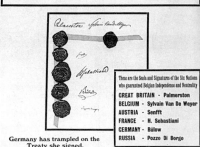

These are the Seals and Signatures of the Six Nations who guaranteed Belgian Independence and Neutrality

GREAT BRITAIN - Palmerston
BELGIUM - Sylvain Van De Weyer
AUSTRIA - Senfft
FRANCE - H. Sebastiani
GERMANY - Bülow
RUSSIA - Pozzo Di Borgo

Germany has trampled on the Treaty she signed.

The 1839 treaty, the 'scrap of paper' guaranteeing Belgian neutrality.

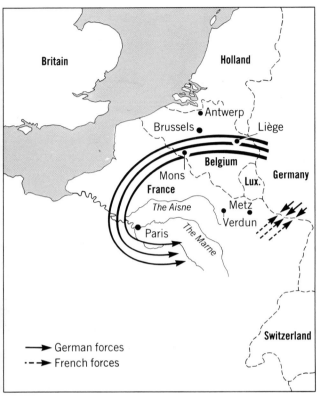

Map 1: The Schlieffen Plan – the theory.

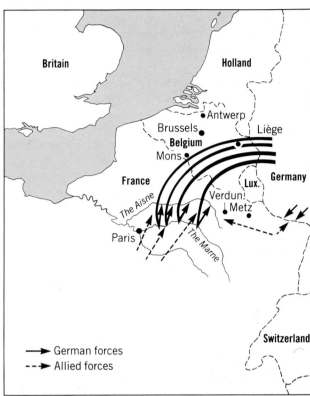

Map 2: The Schlieffen Plan – the reality.

The dead after the Battle of the Marne.

Yet the Allied resistance could do no more than delay the advance of the huge German army. By 4 September the Germans were in sight of Paris. The capital was not taken, however. Instead the Germans departed from their plan and drove east of Paris. As they did so they met the French army marching west from the Metz area in an attempt to cut them off.

The Battle of the Marne

For almost exactly a month the Germans had pushed forward, often marching up to fifty miles a day. Now they faced an Allied counter-attack. The **Battle of the Marne** (5–11 September) was to prove a turning point in history. Under brilliant blue skies nearly two million men struggled for almost a week along a front over two hundred kilometres wide. The French even ferried men from Paris to the battlefront in taxis – a fleet of 250 taxis shuttled back and forth throughout the week, taking fresh men to fight the exhausted Germans. By 11 September the Germans had retreated 60 kilometres to the river Aisne, where they built machine-gun posts and dug trenches to defend themselves.

The great advance had been stopped. Von Moltke informed the Kaiser: 'Your Majesty, we have lost the war.' The fighting, however, was far from over.

2.1 PROPAGANDA

EVIDENCE

To win a major war, a nation needs not only strong armed forces but also the unswerving support of its people. Only with such support can it rely on its workers to produce vital equipment and supplies and on its citizens to go without everyday necessities. In 1914 the Allies – Britain, France and Russia – set about convincing their people that the Germans were evil and had to be stopped. If their people believed this they knew that they would have little difficulty recruiting men for the armed forces or getting volunteers for such work as nursing and ambulance driving. The method they used was **propaganda**. This involved the careful selection of information so that only bad things were reported about the enemy. Often stories were wildly exaggerated to make the enemy appear even worse. From there it was only a short step to actually making up stories to show how evil the enemy was. By the end of 1914 it was widely believed in Britain that the German armies in Belgium were bayoneting babies. German soldiers, too, were continually told that the Allies were carrying out terrible acts of atrocity. Only when soldiers came face to face with the enemy at the front did they learn the truth.

SOURCE **A**

SOURCE **B**

Australian poster issued in 1915. The Huns ransacked Rome in AD 451. ▼

WOUNDED AND A PRISONER OUR SOLDIER CRIES FOR WATER.

THE GERMAN "SISTER" POURS IT ON THE GROUND BEFORE HIS EYES.

THERE IS NO WOMAN IN BRITAIN WHO WOULD DO IT.

THERE IS NO WOMAN IN BRITAIN WHO WILL FORGET IT.

British poster issued early in the war.

EVIDENCE

SOURCE **C**

Daddy, what did YOU do in the Great War?

British recruiting poster.

SOURCE **D**

Which Picture would Your Father like to show his friends?

Australian recruiting poster.

SOURCE **E**

◀ United States recruiting poster.

EXERCISE

1 In what ways are Sources A and B similar?

2 In what ways are Sources C and D similar?

3 Which of the other sources is Source E most like? Explain your answer.

4 The sources in this unit are all examples of propaganda. They were created to make people think and act in certain ways, not necessarily to tell the truth. Does this mean a historian studying the First

World War will not find them useful? Give reasons for your answer.

5 What evidence would you need to decide whether posters were a successful form of propaganda during the First World War?

6 Since these sources come from a variety of countries, they prove that everyone hated the Germans in 1914. Explain why you agree or disagree with this statement.

2.2 THE WESTERN FRONT – WEAPONS AND WARFARE

The Schlieffen Plan had failed, and the German advance came to a halt. There now followed a race to the sea as the Germans, the French and the British Expeditionary Force all dashed north in an attempt to get round the side of the opposing forces. The race was won by neither side but brought heavy casualties. In a fierce battle at **Ypres** in November 1914 the British, French and German armies lost close to a quarter of a million men.

Having failed to advance, the armies began to dig **trenches** to protect their positions from enemy attack. By the end of 1914 these trenches stretched from the Channel coast in Belgium to the mountains in Switzerland. This band of trenches, over six hundred kilometres long, became known as the **Western Front**. For a period of four years casualties were enormous, as both sides tried in vain to push the enemy back. Von Schlieffen had planned for a war of rapid movement; on the Western Front it had now become a war of stalemate.

The trench system

The trenches that the British dug were generally made up of three lines (see Source C). In the **front line** the trenches were usually two metres deep and almost as wide. Men would walk on wooden duck-boards to avoid the mud, and they used a fire-step to position themselves to fire at the enemy. Sandbags protected the top of the trench. In front of this stood coils of barbed wire to trap those enemy soldiers who made it across no man's land, the area between the German and Allied lines. In no man's land were the shallow dug-outs known as 'forlorn hope'. These were occupied by night in the hope of gaining advantage the next day. Rest for the frontline soldier would come from snatched moments of sleep in the dug-outs.

Behind the front line were the **support trenches** and then, further back, **reserve trenches**. Linking the three lines was a series of communication trenches. There were also 'blind alleys' dug to confuse the enemy in case of a successful attack. The whole of the trench system was made to zigzag so as to prevent the enemy firing down the line of the trenches if they were captured. An infantry battalion would usually spend a fortnight rotating

SOURCE B

How the trenches were constructed.

Barbed wire
Sandbags
Ammunition shelf
Dug-out
Duck boards
Fire step
Sump

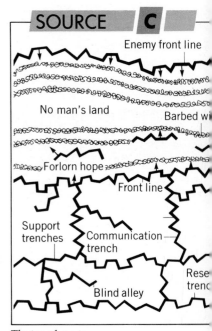

SOURCE C

The trench system.

Enemy front line
No man's land
Barbed wi
Forlorn hope
Front line
Support trenches
Communication trench
Blind alley
Rese trenc

SOURCE A

◄ British machine gunners at the Somme in 1916. Note the use of gas masks.

Artillery guns on the way to the front.

'Propped up against the wall was a dozen men – all gassed. Their colours were black, green and blue, tongues hanging out and eyes staring. One or two were dead and others beyond human aid; some were coughing up green froth from their lungs. As we advanced we passed many more gassed men lying in the ditches and gutterways.'

Lance Sergeant Elmer Cotton, Northumberland Fusiliers, describing a gas attack on Whit Monday 1915.

between the three lines of trenches and the billets behind the line. But if troops were in short supply, they might spend a month or more at the front before being relieved.

Although most soldiers lived in fear of being ordered to charge on enemy trenches ('going over the top'), the daily life in the trenches was often more miserable and tedious than dangerous (see page 18). The fortunate soldier would find himself stationed in a quiet area of the trenches and not at the front during a period of heavy fighting. His day would consist of a routine of sentry duty, trench maintenance and weapon cleaning. If he was really lucky the only action he might see would come during the morning and evening 'hate' periods when both sides would fire at the enemy for several minutes – a grim reminder that death was never far away.

Weapons

The trenches were very strong defences and very difficult to attack. As the war progressed, various weapons were used in a bid to end the stalemate on the Western Front.

The average soldier still carried his rifle and bayonet, with hand grenades for support; but these were of limited use until he had crossed no man's land. The weapon which the generals considered most effective in the trenches was the **artillery gun**. These guns varied from small field-pieces to giant howitzers which could fire shells into enemy lines from a distance of up to 13 kilometres. Despite a shell shortage in 1915, the British fired over 170 million artillery shells in the four years of the war. An artillery bombardment was supposed to destroy the enemy trenches and allow an easy crossing of no man's land (see pages 20–1). Often, however, it did no more than churn up the ground and make no man's land even harder to cross.

The most effective weapon on the Western Front proved to be the **machine gun**. The British thought little of it at the start of the war, but the Germans were much more enthusiastic and used it to great effect against the Allies. Soon the lesson was learned, and both sides had plentiful supplies of machine guns. More than any other weapon, the machine gun led to stalemate on the Western Front. Since attacks against enemy machine gunners produced appalling casualties, the troops were kept pinned in the trenches until ways could be found to reduce the effectiveness of the machine guns.

On 22 April 1915 during the Second Battle of Ypres, the Germans used another new weapon: gas. Hundreds of their French opponents died from suffocation by chlorine gas. Phosgene gas also caused suffocation, but mustard gas was even more painful. It ate away at the lungs and left men crying out in agony as they died slowly. Fortunately the effects of gas attacks could be limited by the issue of gas masks to all soldiers. So, as the war progressed, the attacks became much less frequent.

Perhaps the most significant development in weapons in the First World War came with the introduction of the **tank**. Its use and effectiveness in the war are discussed on pages 50–1.

2.3 TRENCH WARFARE

EVIDENCE

There are many different sorts of sources available to the historian of the First World War. They range from official government publications to reminiscences of old soldiers. The problem the historian faces is to decide which of these sources provide reliable information.

SOURCE

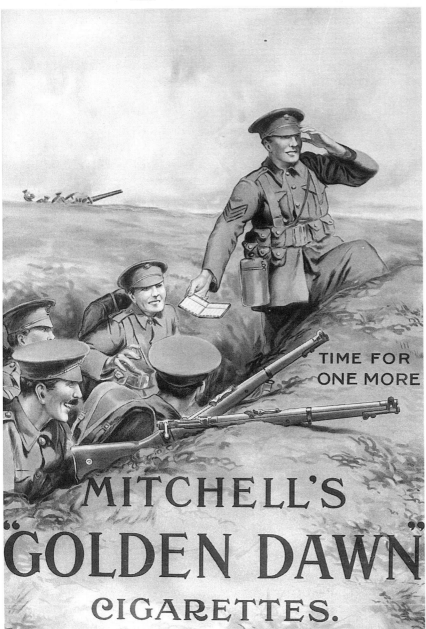

TIME FOR
ONE MORE

MITCHELL'S
"GOLDEN DAWN"
CIGARETTES.

Advertising poster issued in 1915.

SOURCE

A Call
from
the Trenches.

(Extract from a letter from the Trenches.)

"I SAW a recruiting advertisement in a paper the other day. I wonder if the men are responding properly —they would if they could see what the Germans have done in Belgium. And, after all, it's not so bad out here—cold sometimes, and the waiting gets on our nerves a bit, but we are happy and as fit as fiddles. I wonder if————has joined, he certainly ought to."

Does "————" refer to you?

If so

ENLIST TO-DAY.

God Save the King.

Recruiting advertisement in 'The Times', 15 April 1915.

SOURCE C

◀ *Painting of the trench area by C. R. W. Nevison.*

SOURCE D

British soldiers photographed in the trenches, 1916.

SOURCE E

'It is noon now, and some of them are blowing on hot tea to cool it, or eating out of their dixies a hot stew of meat, potatoes and peas. The day is fine and other men are asleep, basking like cats on little sunny shelves and bunks cunningly sculptured out of the trenches' firm clay walls. One little knot of men off duty are bending over a comic paper.'

C.E. Montague describes his experiences in the trenches, 'The Front Line', 1917.

SOURCE F

'You can't possibly picture to yourself what such a battlefield looks like. It is impossible to describe it, and even now, when it is a day behind us, I myself can hardly believe that such bestial barbarity and unspeakable suffering are possible. Every foot of ground churned up a yard deep by the heaviest shells; dead animals; houses and churches so utterly destroyed by shell fire that they can never be of any use again.'

Description of the battle area by a German soldier, 5 November 1914.

EXERCISE

1 a What idea of life in the trenches is given by Source A?

b 'Source A is merely an advertisement designed to sell cigarettes; therefore it has no value to the historian.' Do you agree? Explain your answer.

2 a In what way is the idea of life in the trenches given in Source B similar to that given in Source A?

b What use would you expect a historian to make of Source B?

3 Source C is a painting of the trench area. No date has been given for the painting. Does this matter to a historian?

4 'Source D is a photograph of the trenches. Since the camera never lies, we now know what the trenches must have looked like.' Explain whether you agree or disagree with this statement.

5 What impression of life in the trenches is given by:
a Source E?
b Source F?
c Why do Sources E and F give such a different impression?

6 'Only sources which are not biased are useful to a historian.' Do you agree? Explain your answer, giving examples from this unit.

2.4 LIFE IN THE TRENCHES

EMPATHY

For many men, their period in the trenches was the worst time of their lives. Was this true of all soldiers?

SOURCE A

The road to the front. Beyond this lay the trenches.

SOURCE B

Australians in a front-line trench, May 1916.

SOURCE C

'There was a danger of trench feet, and the men had to rub a sort of fat or whale oil on their feet to prevent it. Lots of the blighters avoided doing that because they knew that if they got trench feet they would be sent back down the line.'

Sergeant J. Haddock, quoted in N. Jones, 'The War Walk', 1983.

SOURCE D

'To add to the general discomfort, the trenches were alive with rats. The knowledge that the gigantic trench rats had grown fat through feeding on the dead bodies in no man's land made the soldiers hate them more fiercely than almost anything else.'

S. Case, 'The First World War', 1976.

EMPATHY

SOURCE E

'I sat in a quiet corner of a barn, de-lousing myself as best I could. The things lay in the seams of trousers, in the deep furrows of long thick woolly pants, and seemed impregnable in their deep entrenchments. A lighted candle applied where they were at their thickest made them pop like Chinese crackers. After a session of this, my face would be covered with small spots from extra big fellows which had popped too vigorously.'

G. Coppard, 'With a Machine Gun to Cambrai', 1969.

SOURCE F

'After breakfast, the routine of the day went on. There was not long to wait before an officer appeared with details of the soldiers' duties for the day. Weapon cleaning and inspection, always an important task, would soon be followed by pick-and-shovel work. Trench maintenance went on all the time, a job without end. The carrying of rations and supplies from the rear also went on all the time.'

T. Howarth, 'On the Western Front', 1976.

SOURCE G

'The dead man lay on the earth. Never before had I seen a man who had just been killed. His face and body were terribly gashed and the smell of blood, mixed with the fumes of the shell, made me sick. Only a great effort stopped my legs giving way, and a voice seemed to whisper in my ear. "Why shouldn't you be next?"'

A First World War soldier remembers his first sight of death.

SOURCE H

'It's the Saxons that's across the road. They're quiet fellows, the Saxons; they don't want to fight any more than we do. So there's a kind of understanding between us. Don't fire at us and we'll not fire at you.'
[The Saxons were from the region of Germany called Saxony.]

Comments of a soldier in the trenches, quoted in P. MacGill, 'The Red Horizon', 1916.

EXERCISE

1 When soldiers were afflicted with trench foot they suffered great pain. Yet Source C suggests that they might have infected themselves deliberately. Do you believe what Source C says? Explain your answer.

2 Source F describes part of the daily routine of a trench soldier. Sometimes this routine would be followed for days on end.
  a Choose from the following list the description which you think would best sum up a trench soldier's view of such a routine and give reasons for your choice:

'I like it. It's very interesting.'
'Why can't I do some proper soldiering? I joined the army to kill the enemy.'
'Anything is better than fighting.'
  b Do you think that all the soldiers would have felt the same way? Explain your answer.

3 In 1915 a British newspaper printed a letter from a lady reader who claimed: 'The women will tolerate no such cry as "peace".' Do you think the soldiers in the trenches would have agreed with this view?

2.5 STALEMATE ON THE WESTERN FRONT

In 1914 it was confidently believed that the war would be fought between quick-moving armies and that 'it would all be over by Christmas'. At the start of 1915, however, there were millions of men dug into strong positions in trenches, facing equally strong positions on the other side of no man's land. Far from being a war of movement, the war on the Western Front had become one of **stalemate**. Britain's army leader, **Lord Kitchener**, was as puzzled as his generals about how to win the war. He admitted: 'I don't know what is to be done. This isn't war.'

While the generals were unsure about how to win the war, many of them believed that final victory could only be won on the Western Front. So they were prepared to pour huge numbers of troops into the area in an effort to make the all-important breakthrough. The British army was swelled by millions of **volunteers** responding to the government's call to enlist, and the French had even more troops at their disposal. (In France men were **conscripted** – that is, ordered by the Government to join the army.) With such enormous numbers, surely a breakthrough could be achieved?

No such breakthrough was ever made. Instead, during 1915–16 there was slaughter previously unknown in the history of warfare. The theory was simple: artillery shells would batter the enemy trenches, and then the infantry would cross no man's land and wipe out any remaining enemy forces. The consequences were tragic. Hundreds of thousands of men were killed or wounded, and very little territory was gained by either side.

Soon, however, there were other calculations to be considered. Perhaps the war could be won by a policy of **attrition** – that is by wearing the enemy down so that their supplies of men and equipment were used up before yours were. Politicians and generals began to calculate whether a battle would bring more losses for the enemy than for their own armies. If it did, it was considered to be helping win the war.

Despite the appalling losses of 1915, the Allied commanders were still confident that a breakthrough could be made. The French commander-in-chief, **General Joffre**, and his British counterpart, **Sir Douglas Haig**, agreed on a full-scale attack along the **river Somme** in the summer of 1916. The first half of the year was to be spent in building up supplies of men and munitions.

The Battle of Verdun

The Germans also had plans for a major attack in 1916. German successes on the Eastern Front (see page 22) had enabled them to transfer half a million soldiers to the Western Front. The German commander, **General Falkenhayn**, proposed to use his new troops in an attack on the French fortress of **Verdun**. He had little interest in taking the fortress but was more interested in how many casualties he could inflict. His aim was to 'bleed the French white'.

Falkenhayn had chosen his target well. The French generals had removed most of Verdun's guns and used them elsewhere on the Front. They were not convinced that it was important enough to

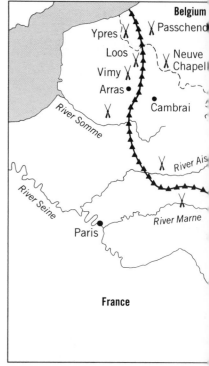

The Western Front, 1914–16.

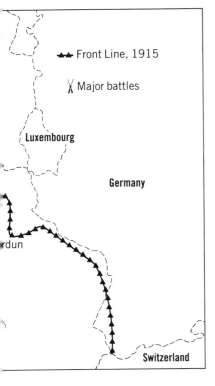

Front Line, 1915

Major battles

Luxembourg

Germany

dun

Switzerland

the war effort to suffer heavy losses in defending it. Verdun, however, was not just a fortress. It held a special place in French history as an impregnable stronghold against all attacks. In many ways Verdun was the symbol of France's military power. Prime Minister Briand angrily informed his generals: 'You may not think losing Verdun to be a defeat, but everyone else will. If you surrender Verdun, I'll dismiss the lot of you.' So it was that the French decided that Verdun must not fall.

The Germans began their attack by firing two million shells from over 1,400 artillery guns on the hills around Verdun. Soon two of the thirteen forts defending Verdun were in German hands. The French placed **General Pétain** in charge of defending Verdun; his famous comment, *'Ils ne passeront pas'* ('They shall not pass'), gave great hope to the French defenders. Yet what Verdun needed as much as the courage of the French troops was supplies. Within a week of the battle only one road was open to the city, and down this single road ('the Sacred Way') lorries shuttled supplies at the rate of one every fourteen seconds.

Despite these efforts, by July 1916 Verdun was close to falling into German hands. Joffre would still not hear of surrender, since he knew that the British were about to launch a major attack along the Somme which would divert German troops from Verdun. In mid-July the Germans called off their attack. They had not captured Verdun but they had certainly succeeded in inflicting enormous casualties on the French. What they had not planned for was the severity of their own casualties (see Source C).

The German offensive had caused losses of close to a million men. Never before had there been such slaughter. Yet incredibly these figures were to be surpassed even before the year was out, for on 1 July the long-awaited **Somme offensive** was finally launched (see pages 24–5).

SOURCE B

Month	Battle	Country	Casualties
January	Compiègne	French	90,000
March	Neuve Chapelle	British	11,000
May	Arras	French	120,000
May	Aubers	British	17,000
September	Loos	British	60,000

The cost of Anglo-French offensives, 1915.

SOURCE C

Estimated losses at Verdun – killed, wounded or missing

French	542,000
German	434,000

From J. Ray, 'The First World War', 1975.

◀ *Casualties of war – a grim reminder of the realities of the Western Front.*

2.6 THE EASTERN FRONT, 1914–15

In the west the German plan to defeat France in a matter of weeks had failed. **Russia** was determined that the Germans should be even more unsuccessful in the east. The Russians aimed to strike while the Germans were engaged in attacking France, and on 10 August 1914 the order went out to begin 'the quickest possible advance against Germany, by attacking those forces Germany had left behind in East Prussia'. The Germans had expected the Russians to take six weeks to fully mobilize their forces; but within ten days of the outbreak of war four Russian armies were on the move. The Russian 'problem' was to prove even more annoying than the delay encountered in crossing Belgium.

The Schlieffen Plan had relied on the armies of Austria keeping the Russians pinned down. According to plan the Austrians had launched a full-scale attack on Russia in August and had quickly taken control of a large number of towns and villages. They soon found, however, that the Russians were stronger than they anticipated. By the end of 1914 the Austrian advance had not only been halted; it had been reversed. During a spell of four days the Russians advanced two hundred kilometres. The Austrians retreated in disarray as thousands of their men deserted, and much of their equipment was left behind.

Further north the Russians were equally successful. Their First and Second Armies drove into East Prussia and caused panic among the depleted German forces. Because of the vast size of Russia's population, some people thought its army was unstoppable and talked of the Russian '**steamroller**' – slow to move but almost impossible to stop. There were even those who predicted that the Russians would continue to advance until they reached Berlin.

In response to the Russian threat, the Kaiser was forced to call **Field Marshal von Hindenburg** out of retirement, and two divisions were transferred from the west. At the end of August, Hindenburg's forces met one of the two invading armies in a five-day battle at **Tannenberg**. By skilful manoeuvring the Germans trapped the Russians in swampland. Many of the 125,000 Russian deaths came by drowning. Rather than face the disgrace of defeat, the Russian commander, General Samsonov, rode into the woods and shot himself. One week later the Germans slaughtered a further 100,000 Russian troops at the **Battle of the Masurian Lakes**. Germany was no longer at risk. Now it was Russia which was threatened.

The threat to Russia became even more serious in 1915. In the spring the Germans sent reinforcements to help the Austrians in **Galicia**. Within two months they had driven the Russians out of the province and were advancing into Russia once more. In the north the Germans followed up the two great victories of 1915 by pushing the Russians deep into their own territory. The advance was stopped by the arrival of winter, but it seemed a real possibility that 1916 would see Russia being driven out of the war.

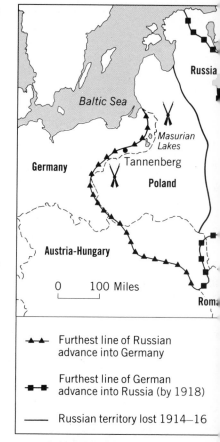

Furthest line of Russian advance into Germany

Furthest line of German advance into Russia (by 1918)

Russian territory lost 1914–16

The Eastern Front, 1914–16.

 SOURCE **A**

Russian prisoners under Austrian guard, 1915. ▶

SOURCE B

'The sight of thousands of Russians driven into two huge lakes or swamps to drown was ghastly. So fearful was the sight of these thousands of men, with their guns, horses and ammunition, struggling in the water, that to shorten their agony, they turned the machine guns on them. But even in spite of that there was movement seen among them for a week after.'

General von Moltke describing the German slaughter of the Russians at Tannenberg.

One of the major causes of the Russian defeats on the Eastern Front was **poor organization**. Russia had over six million troops in 1914 but found it almost impossible to supply them. At one time the Russian army was using more artillery shells each day than Russia's factories could produce in a month. There were not even enough rifles to go round, and men sometimes had to wait until their fellow soldiers were killed in battle before they could get a rifle.

Yet, despite these difficulties, the Russians were making a major contribution to the Allied war effort. Although they were in retreat, they were keeping substantial numbers of German and Austrian troops pinned down. As 1915 closed, the Allies began to consider what might be done to help the Russians.

SOURCE C

German cavalry passing through a Russian village, January 1916.

SOURCE D

'In several infantry regiments which have taken part in the recent battles at least one-third of the men had no rifle. These poor devils had to wait patiently under a shower of shrapnel, until their comrades fell before their eyes and they could pick up their arms.'

Russian chief of staff, 1915.

2.7 **THE SOMME: DISASTER FROM DAY ONE**

CAUSATION

On 1 July 1916 the British launched a major offensive along the **river Somme**. Before the attack there was a seven-day artillery bombardment of the German trenches which was so loud that it could be heard in London. For almost thirty kilometres the British guns stood side by side firing over a million and a half shells into the German trenches. Two-thirds of the shells contained shrapnel in the form of small lead pellets. These shells were designed to destroy the barbed wire in front of the German trenches.

The British commander-in-chief, Sir Douglas Haig, doubted that there would be 'even a rat' alive in the German trenches. Yet for many of Haig's men the Somme was their last battle. During the barrage the Germans had been sheltering in specially reinforced dug-outs. When the shelling stopped, they raced to their normal trench positions. As one German soldier commented: 'The British were coming – slowly.' As the British infantry advanced at a walking pace, the German machine guns opened fire on them with devastating effect. How could such a disaster have occurred?

SOURCE D

	Officers	Soldiers
Killed/died of wounds	993	18,247
Wounded	1,337	34,156
Missing	96	2,056
Taken prisoner	12	573
Total	2,438	55,032

British losses on the first day of the Battle of the Somme.

SOURCE A

A British howitzer in action before the attack.

SOURCE E

One more sad statistic: British soldier killed on the Somme, September 1916.

SOURCE B

'He said, "You'll find the barbed wire in front of the German trenches blown away." Blown away! Nothing of the sort! It was as solid as anything. That was the whole trouble. Wrong information.'

Jack Cousins, 7th Bedfordshire Regiment commenting years later in a television interview on orders received before the attack.

SOURCE C

'A large proportion of the heavy guns available were of obsolete pattern and poor range, while much of the ammunition was defective. Thus the shells could not penetrate the dug-outs in which the German machine gunners were sheltering – in waiting.'

B. H. Liddel Hart, 'History of the First World War', 1972.

SOURCE F

'British security surrounding the Somme offensive was by no means perfect. Among other indiscretions, the press reported a speech made by a member of the government requesting workers in munition factories not to question why the Whitsun Bank Holiday was being suspended. A German army commander commented that it was "the surest proof that there will be a great British offensive before long". For several weeks the German defenders had industriously practised rushing their machine guns out from the dug-outs. This had been perfected to a three-minute drill.'

A.J.P. Taylor, 'The Twentieth Century', 1979.

SOURCE G

A British soldier's opinion of the instructions to cross no man's land at a slow walking pace:

'Whether they did this on purpose to show how lucky we were and had nothing to fear, whether they did it to cheer us up or whether they really thought they were correct, I don't know. But they made a huge mistake; a wicked mistake. There's no doubt about that.'

Russell Bradshaw, 11th East Lancashire Regiment.

SOURCE H

'The necessity of crossing no man's land at a good pace, so as to reach the parapet before the enemy could reach it, was not discussed. Each man carried 66 lb – over half his body weight – which made it difficult to get out of a trench, impossible to move much quicker than a slow walk or to rise or lay down quickly.'

B. H. Liddell Hart 'History of the First World War', 1972.

EXERCISE

1 **a** Do you think that the attack on the first day of the Somme offensive would have been more successful if the British artillery had worked better?

b Do you think the attack on the first day would have been more successful if the German barbed wire had been cut into small pieces?

c Do you think that the attack on the first day would have been more successful if a member of the British government had not hinted that a major attack would soon be launched?

d Do you think that the attack on the first day would have been more successful if the British soldiers had run across no man's land?

2 Which of the reasons given in question 1 do you think was the most important cause of the British failure on the first day of the Somme offensive?

3 'General Haig was a highly respected general who was very popular with his fellow officers. He therefore couldn't have devised a bad plan.' Explain whether you agree or disagree with this statement.

4 Would you agree that every time something goes wrong in history it is always someone's fault? Try to use the events on the first day of the Somme offensive to explain your answer.

2.8 GALLIPOLI AND THE DARDANELLES

In October 1914 **Turkey** joined the war on the side of the Central Powers (Germany and Austria-Hungary). For some years Turkey had been on friendly terms with Germany, and the Germans had helped build up the Turkish armed forces. In October 1914 those forces were used to bombard the Russian town of Sebastopol, and in December a Turkish army 95,000 strong drove into Russia.

The Russians dealt easily with the attack, but the Turkish intervention in the war presented the Allies with a serious problem. Since Turkey controlled the entrance to the Black Sea (a narrow strait known as **the Dardanelles**), supplies could no longer be sent to Russia through the Mediterranean. Some Allied leaders – especially **Winston Churchill**, the British First Lord of the Admiralty, thought that an attack should be made on Turkey. This idea gained support as the Allies began to realize that the war on the Western Front had reached stalemate. If the Germans could not be defeated there, then an attack would have to be launched where it would harm the German war effort.

Churchill therefore devised a plan to land troops on the **Gallipoli Peninsula** at the entrance to the Dardanelles. Once this was taken, the straits could be cleared of the forts and mines which had blocked the route to the Black Sea. The Turkish capital, Constantinople, could then be attacked, and the Turks forced out of the war. Once Allied military superiority had been shown in the area, then perhaps some of the neighbouring neutral countries, such as Bulgaria and Greece, would join the war on the Allied side. This would make Allied forces much too strong for Austria, forcing the Austrians out of the war. Germany would then be left to fight on its own. This was an ambitious plan and could have won the war for the Allies. Yet it was to be a miserable failure and led to Churchill resigning in disgrace.

SOURCE A

'How lucky they are to escape Flanders and the trenches and be sent to the "gorgeous east".'

Prime Minister Asquith referring to British troops sent to Gallipoli, February 1915.

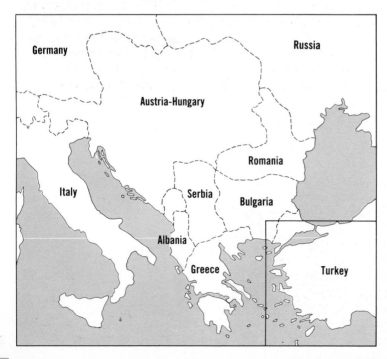

The Dardanelles Campaign. ▼

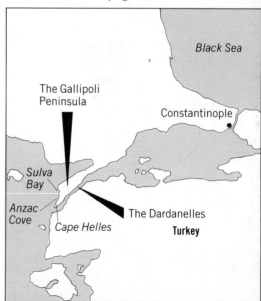

SOURCE B

'The whole beach went up in flames in front of us. Bullets hit us like a blizzard of lead. The boat next to us was torn apart – bodies, blood, splinters of wood. Bodies jammed so tight in other small boats they couldn't even fall over.'

New Zealand soldier describing the landing at Anzac Cove.

SOURCE C

Allied losses in the Dardanelles Campaign

Total losses	213,980
Losses from sickness	145,154
Including:	
Dysentry	29,728
Frostbite	15,000
Diarrhoea	10,373
Enteric fever	9,423

SOURCE D

The attacks began in February 1915 when four Turkish forts at the entrance to the straits were bombarded and destroyed by British and French warships. But it was nearly a month before the attack was followed up with an operation against the inner forts. During the delay the Turks strengthened their position, and the operation ended in failure. Three battleships were sunk by mines, and more than three hundred men were lost.

It was now decided that an Allied army should be landed on the beaches of Gallipoli to capture the forts guarding the entrance to the straits and allow them to be cleared of mines. On 25 April a force of **Anzacs** (men of the Australian and New Zealand Army Corps) were landed at a bay now called Anzac Cove. They had never practised landing on enemy beaches, and their commander, Sir Ian Hamilton, did not even have up-to-date maps of the area!

The Turks were waiting for the attack. Thousands of the Anzac forces were mown down by machine-gun fire. The troops secured a foothold on the beach but were unable to advance further. They were forced to 'dig in' to protect themselves. Soon the Gallipoli beaches looked like a miniature version of the Western Front. On 6 August a further landing was made by Anzac forces at Sulva Bay. This time the Anzacs landed almost unopposed. But two days later they tried to advance, met fierce resistance and were forced to dig trenches to defend their position.

The Dardanelles campaign had been planned to end the stalemate on the Western Front. Now it too had resulted in trench warfare and stalemate. Yet, unlike on the Western Front, here the Anzacs had heat, water shortage and disease to deal with. There were more Allied casualties from sickness during the campaign than from Turkish bullets. During November there was also a blizzard which inflicted thousands of casualties through frostbite.

By December 1915 it was obvious that the campaign had failed. Hamilton was dismissed and replaced by General Monro, whose job was to organize the withdrawal. Between 10 December and 9 January 1916 over 135,000 troops were evacuated without a single loss of life. It was a brilliant end to a miserable campaign.

◄ *One of the clever ideas to cover the evacuation: water from the top tin drops into the bottom tin and fires the gun.*

3.1 THE CONTRIBUTION OF THE EMPIRE

EVIDENCE

When Britain declared war on Germany it committed more than just its own citizens to war. The huge **British Empire** comprised of over 400 million subjects, and they too were now part of the First World War. Yet Britain could not compel all its subjects to join the war. Four of Britain's colonies – Canada, New Zealand, South Africa and Australia – were known as **Dominions** and had their own governments. They could legally refuse to give their active support. They did not. In 1919 the Empire could look back with pride at the contribution it had made in bringing about an Allied victory.

SOURCE A

▼ *British recruiting poster, 1915.*

SOURCE B

'Altogether about 120,000 New Zealanders saw active service, of whom about 17,000 were killed – a vast number of young men whose loss was severely felt in the difficult inter-war years. Despite the smallness of her population and her distance from Europe, New Zealand's contribution to the Allied victory was far from negligible.'

A.J.P. Taylor in 'The Twentieth Century', 1979.

SOURCE C

Indian poster appealing for support to fight the war.

SOURCE D

'They played a part of such distinction that thenceforward they were marked out as storm troops: for the remainder of the war they were brought along to head the assault in one great battle after another. Whenever the Germans found the Canadian Corps coming into the line, they prepared for the worst.'

British Prime Minister, Lloyd George, commenting on the bravery of the Canadians after the Battle of the Somme.

SOURCE E

An illustration from a book written by an Anzac soldier.

SOURCE G

'As the first enthusiasm faded, recruiting figures dropped rapidly. Whereas in June 1915, for example, recruits had numbered over 12,000, a year later the figure was little more than half that. By 1917 recruiting figures had dropped to below half the figure of 7,000 a year considered necessary.'

A. J. P. Taylor, discussing Australian recruitment in 'The Twentieth Century', 1979.

SOURCE H

'Dauntlessly, tirelessly, they accomplished their purpose. Thousands of stalwart men from Canada and the vast lands under the Southern Cross had unflinchingly laid down their lives. The Colonies had always shared our history, but now they had made a history of their own.'

'The Times', 26 May 1919.

SOURCE F

◀ *West Indian troops on active service in France.*

EXERCISE

1 In what ways does Source A suggest that in 1915 Britain believed that the Empire was making a valuable contribution to the war?

2 Source B is a secondary source. Does this mean that it will be of less value to a historian than a primary source?

3 a Does Source C prove that India made a valuable contribution to the Allied victory?
  b Does Source F prove that the West Indies made a valuable contribution to the Allied victory?

4 'Source E is an illustration from a book written by an Anzac soldier. It is bound to be biased.'
  a Explain whether you agree or disagree with this statement.
  b If it is biased does that mean it has no value to the historian?

5 Does Source G show that the Australians weren't really very interested in helping Britain?

6 Source H comments on the contribution of the Empire in the war.
  a Which parts of Source H could be described as:
    i) Fact
    ii) Opinion?
  b How would you go about trying to prove that the comments you have labelled as 'fact' are correct?
  c Should opinion be regarded as of no value to a historian?

CHANGE

3.2 CHANGING ATTITUDES TO WAR

In 1914 Europe had been gripped by a form of 'war madness'. Men flocked to join the armed forces before it was too late. The war would not last long, and there was glory to be won. In France, Britain and Germany alike popular opinion was behind the war, and politicians called on their people to 'do their bit'. For many it was a time of relief. The historian Malcolm Brown talks of how his father met a friend in the street, who told him: 'Well, it's come at last!' Yet it was not long before soldiers returning to Britain on leave were complaining of the 'war madness that runs wild everywhere'.

The soldiers' dissatisfaction was seen in both the British and French armies. In 1917 there was a serious **mutiny** at the British base in Etaples and in the same year French soldiers mutinied. The French mutinies followed the failure of a huge offensive launched by **General Nivelle** (see pages 48–9) and may have involved as many as 35,000 men. Few soldiers finished the war with the same enthusiasm with which they had started it.

SOURCE E

The execution of a French mutineer, 1917.

SOURCE A

'We felt that time was slipping away. At any moment there might be a decisive battle on land or sea, the war would end, and we would be late for the hunt.'

A British soldier remembers hearing that he was to be stationed in England instead of being sent to France in 1914.

SOURCE C

The French mutinies of 1917

Total number of French divisions	112
Profoundly affected	5
Very seriously affected	6
Seriously affected	15
Affected by repeated incidents	25
Affected by one incident only	17
Total affected	68

From 'The Marshall Cavendish Illustrated Encyclopaedia of World War One', 1984.

SOURCE F

SOURCE B

'It seemed as though the whole French army was gathered there for a victorious assault. The air was filled with enthusiasm, and a heroic mood prevailed in each of us. Officers and soldiers refused to go on leave so as not to miss the great offensive.'

A French soldier recalls the eve of Nivelle's offensive in 1917.

SOURCE D

'Towards the end of the war, we were so fed up we wouldn't even sing "God Save the King" on church parade. Never mind the bloody King we used to say, he was safe enough; it should have been God save us.'

Private J. A. Hooper, 7th Green Howards Regiment.

CHANGE

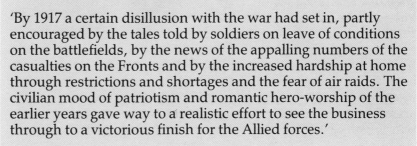

SOURCE G

'By 1917 a certain disillusion with the war had set in, partly encouraged by the tales told by soldiers on leave of conditions on the battlefields, by the news of the appalling numbers of the casualties on the Fronts and by the increased hardship at home through restrictions and shortages and the fear of air raids. The civilian mood of patriotism and romantic hero-worship of the earlier years gave way to a realistic effort to see the business through to a victorious finish for the Allied forces.'

Scottish Record Office 'The First World War', 1986.

A French drawing of 1917. Entitled 'The Grumble', it shows the discontent of the French soldiers. ▼

EXERCISE

1 a Why do you think the soldier in Source A was so disappointed to miss being posted in France?

b Do you think he would have said the same thing in 1918?

2 Before 1914 Britain had not fought in a major European war for over fifty years. How might this have affected the feelings of:
a the soldiers in 1914?
b the civilians in 1914?

3 Source F was drawn before Nivelle's offensive in 1917, yet Source B suggests that the French troops were confident and cheerful. Is there any way in which both sources could be correct?

4 Sources C and E tell us that there was mutiny after the failure of Nivelle's offensive. Do you think that this mutiny can all be blamed on the failure of that offensive?

5 The soldiers who wouldn't sing 'God Save the King' in Source D were part of an army which claimed in 1914 that it was fighting for 'King and Country'. Does this mean that they did not like the King any more? If not, why not?

6 a What does Source G tell you about the attitude to war of people at home in 1914?

b In what way had their opinion changed by 1918?

c What reasons are given for the change of attitude?

7 Do you think that it is true to say that in 1914 there was overwhelming support for the war, both at home and at the front, whereas in 1918 everyone wanted it to end? Explain your answer.

3.3 THE WAR AT SEA

At the outbreak of war the British people confidently expected to see a decisive naval victory over the Germans. Yet there was virtually no contact between the two navies until May 1916. Both the British and the Germans had spent huge sums building up mighty fleets and they were reluctant to put them at risk. Since the Kaiser would not risk his High Seas Fleet until he was confident that it was a match for the British, it remained largely inactive in its north German ports. The British were concerned about the threat to their fleet from **submarines and mines**. The first British casualties, the cruiser *Amphion* and the battleship *Audacious*, were both victims of German mines, and in September 1914 three cruisers were sunk by the German submarine *U-9*. It seemed wisest to keep the Grand Fleet in its base at Scapa Flow. From there it would be able to attack the German fleet if it entered the North Sea.

Early skirmishes went Britain's way. In August 1914 the British sank three German light cruisers and one destroyer at the **Battle of Heligoland Bight**. They followed this by sinking the German cruiser *Blücher* at the **Battle of Dogger Bank** in 1915. But in November 1914 the German Admiral von Spee sank two British cruisers at the **Battle of Coronel** off the coast of Chile. The news horrified the British people, but Spee knew that his victory was due to the superiority of his ships over the old British cruisers. Once the British sent modern battle cruisers to gain revenge, the result would be very different. So it proved. In December 1914 Spee's squadron was destroyed, and the Admiral and his sons were among the 2,300 German sailors drowned.

The Battle of Jutland

On 13 May 1916 came the clash that both nations had been waiting for. The two great **Dreadnought** fleets – 259 warships carrying over 100,000 men – met at the **Battle of Jutland**. The German High Seas Fleet had gained a new Admiral, von Scheer. He was keen for a confrontation and sent a squadron of ships under Admiral Hipper into the North Sea to act as bait for the British. He intended to follow close behind and make a surprise attack on the Grand Fleet. The British, however, had broken the German naval code and knew he was coming. They were, therefore, ready for an attack.

Despite the fierce fighting, the casualties were light. Good visibility was of crucial importance, because much of the fighting was at long range. Yet the main fleets did not come into contact until 6.30 p.m. on what was a misty evening. The firing was something of a 'hit-and-miss' affair. Perhaps more worrying for the British was that the German ships proved to be better armoured and less easily damaged than the British. When night fell, the Germans broke off the action and ran for port, although it was the British who had suffered the most damage. The Kaiser argued that the British fleet had finally been defeated; but, since the German fleet never emerged from port again, the British claimed victory. It was a battle both sides could claim to have won.

SOURCE C

A German couple nurse their 'baby' as a smiling Kaiser looks on.

SOURCE D

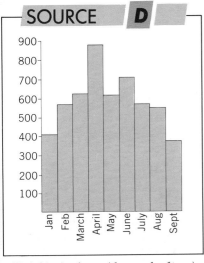

Allied shipping losses (thousands of tons), 1917.

SOURCE E

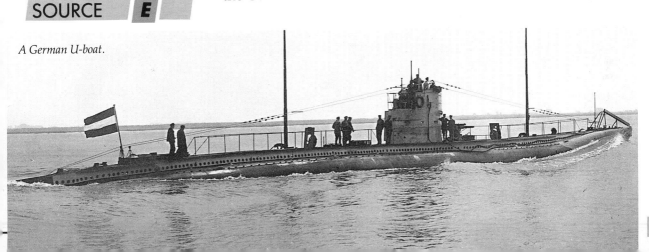

A German U-boat.

Submarines

Despite British claims of victory at Jutland, by 1917 the German **submarines** had brought Britain close to defeat in the war. As an island, Britain relied heavily on its merchant fleet to ferry imports of food and supplies from abroad. The Germans planned to use their U-boats (submarines) to end this trade. In February 1915 Germany announced that all merchant shipping either entering or leaving British waters would be destroyed. It was an ambitious plan, since the Germans had only twenty-one U-boats at the time, and there were often almost 15,000 sailings a week to and from British ports. This campaign of unrestricted U-boat warfare sank only 4 per cent of British capacity during 1915, but it provided a valuable rehearsal for the more determined campaign of 1917. It also caused the sinking of the Cunard liner, *Lusitania* with the loss of 1,198 lives (see pages 34–5). Following a protest by the United States the Germans reduced their indiscriminate sinking of ships.

By 1917, however, the German U-boat fleet had increased steadily (the number reached almost 200 in 1918). Germany felt confident that Britain could be brought to its knees by another campaign of unrestricted warfare. British losses had continued to be high since 1915 despite the introduction of **anti-submarine methods**. The sowing of huge minefields in the English Channel and the introduction of depth charges had hindered the German submarines. So too had the use of 'Q-ships'. These were ships which were armed but disguised to look like merchant vessels. When attacked by U-boats they often gave them a nasty shock.

The 1917 campaign was so successful for the Germans that these measures proved ineffective. Merchant captains left port knowing that one in four ships would not reach their destination. By April 1917 Britain had only six weeks' food supply left. Lord Derby, Secretary of State for War, admitted the government was at 'its wit's end as to how to deal with these submarines'.

Fortunately the answer was at hand. On the insistence of the Prime Minister, Lloyd George, the **convoy system** was introduced. Merchant ships sailed in groups and were protected by Royal Navy destroyers. This idea, coupled with the measures introduced earlier, saved Britain from defeat in the war. Losses dropped dramatically, and the U-boat threat was defeated. It was the Germans who were starved into submission in 1918.

3.4 THE SINKING OF THE *LUSITANIA*

EVIDENCE

SOURCE **A**

On Saturday 1 May 1915 a luxury British liner, the *Lusitania*, left New York. The German Embassy had warned in February 1915 that any ship entering the 'war zone' around Britain or Ireland was liable to be sunk, and some passengers had received anonymous warnings not to sail. Yet the numbers of passengers was a record for the time of year. At 3.10 p.m. on 8 May the *Lusitania* was torpedoed by a German submarine off the coast of Ireland. The ship sank in just eight minutes, and 1,198 passengers were drowned. The *Daily Express* claimed: 'It is simply an act of piracy. Nothing more.' The United States government was so shocked (128 of the passengers were American) that it came near to declaring war on Germany. Had the Germans deliberately murdered innocent passengers? If so, why?

SOURCE **B**

The *Lusitania's* cargo:
- 4,927 boxes of cartridges addressed to the Royal Arsenal at Woolwich.
- 1,248 cases of shrapnel (the firm supplying them to the *Lusitania* described them as '1,248 cases of 3-inch shrapnel shells filled').
- 3,863 boxes of cheese and 696 tubs of butter addressed to a box number in Liverpool. This box number was that used by the Naval Experimental Establishment.

Adapted from J. Hamer, 'The Twentieth Century', 1980.

SOURCE **C**

'Under strict secrecy the *Lusitania* entered dry-dock at Liverpool on 12 May 1913. The shelter deck was adapted to take four 6-inch guns on either side, making a total complement of twelve guns, each firing a shell containing high explosive.'

C. Simpson, 'Lusitania', 1972.

SOURCE **D**

NOTICE!

TRAVELLERS intending to embark on the Atlantic voyage are reminded that a state of war exists between Germany and her allies and Great Britain and her allies; that the zone of war includes the waters adjacent to the British Isles; that, in accordance with formal notice given by the Imperial German Government, vessels flying the flag of Great Britain, or of any of her allies, are liable to destruction in those waters and that travellers sailing in the war zone on ships of Great Britain or her allies do so at their own risk.

IMPERIAL GERMAN EMBASSY,
WASHINGTON, D. C. APRIL 22, 1915.

Warning from the German Embassy printed in US newpapers beside Cunard's advertisement, Saturday 1 May 1915.

SOURCE **E**

BRITISH AND AMERICAN BABIES MURDERED BY THE KAISER

'Daily Mail' headline and photograph, Monday 10 May 1915.

◀ *Artist's impression of the sinking of the 'Lusitania'.*

SOURCE **F**

'Every human life is, of course, valuable and its loss is deplorable. But measured by the methods introduced by our enemies, forcing us to retaliatory measures in self-defence, the death of non-combatants is a matter of no consequence.'

'Frankfurter Zeitung' (a German newspaper), 8 May 1915.

SOURCE **G**

'Whatever the facts regarding the *Lusitania*, the principal fact is that a great steamer, primarily and chiefly a conveyance for passengers, and carrying a thousand souls who had no part or lot in the conduct of the war, was torpedoed and sunk without so much as a challenge or warning and that men, women and children were sent to their death in circumstances unparalleled in modern warfare.'

Official note sent to Germany by the United States government.

EXERCISE

1 How accurate a picture of the sinking of the *Lusitania* do you think is given in Source A?

2 The British government claimed that the *Lusitania* was an unarmed passenger liner. Sources B and C suggest that this was not true.
   a Is there any reason to doubt either of the sources?
   b If Sources B and C are correct, does this mean that the British government was lying, or could it just have been mistaken?

3 'Source D proves that the Germans intended to sink the *Lusitania*.' Explain whether you agree or disagree with this statement.

4 Sources E and F are both from newspapers.
   a Which of the two accounts is likely to be more accurate?
   b Are newspaper accounts reliable sources of historical evidence?

5 Do Sources A to G prove that the Germans had good reason to sink the *Lusitania*? Give reasons for your answer.

3.5 THE WAR IN THE AIR

In 1914 the aeroplane was a very new invention. Neither the Allies nor the Central Powers had many planes – and they were not really sure what to do with the ones they had. The British Expeditionary Force (BEF), for example, had arrived in France with only sixty-three planes. They were part of the **Royal Flying Corps** (RFC), a branch of the British army. At this stage planes were not important enough for there to be a separate 'air force'.

One of the major problems that airmen faced was the **fragile construction** of their machines. They were made of wood and canvas and were held together by piano wire. They had open cockpits with no heating, so pilots had to wear heavy coats and goggles to keep warm. Often they rubbed whale oil into their faces to avoid frostbite. Flying these planes was dangerous, and there were no parachutes to save a pilot if his plane was shot down or, more likely, suffered from mechanical failure.

The first task given to aeroplanes was that of **reconnaissance**. They were especially useful for photographing the movement of enemy armies or locating artillery targets on the Western Front. Sir John French, Commander of the BEF in France, said in September 1914 that the RFC had 'furnished me with complete and accurate information which has been of incalculable value in the conduct of operations.'

As planes developed, so **air combat** between rival aircraft became more common. In early planes pilots had carried pistols and later machine guns. In 1915, however, the Germans perfected the system of **synchronized firing**. This meant that planes could be fitted with machine guns which were synchronized to fire between the revolving propellor blades. The 'dogfights' between opposing pilots have become famous in the history of the war. Each country had its heroic **'aces'** whose exploits were recorded in great detail in their nations' newspapers. Pilots such as Captain **Manfred von Richthofen** ('The Red Baron') fought duels to the death in planes like the British Sopwith Camel, the French Spad and the German Albatross.

It is a myth, however, to see these men as heroes who cared little for their enemies' lives and even less for their own. Captain Albert Ball, who shot down forty-three enemy planes, was killed before reaching even his twenty-first birthday. In one of his last letters he wrote: 'I do get tired of living always to kill and I am really beginning to feel like a murderer. Shall be so pleased when I have finished.'

Bombing methods developed during the war. As early as January 1915 the Germans used **Zeppelins** to bomb England. The Zeppelin was a giant airship filled with hydrogen gas and driven by engines attached underneath. During 1915 Zeppelins made twenty raids on England and killed 188 civilians. The sight of the huge airships hovering almost silently over the towns terrified people. Improved **defence measures**, however, proved very effective. Searchlights linked to better anti-aircraft guns, barrage balloons with cable aprons and, most effectively, night-flying fighters put an end to the Zeppelin threat – though their attacks had caused almost 500 civilian deaths and over 1,200 injuries.

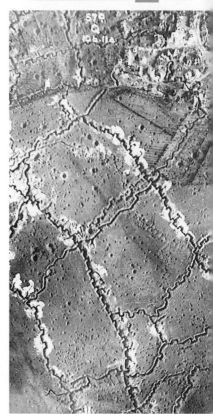

Aircraft for reconnaissance. The trenches as seen from the air.

Pilot	Country	Number of victims
Capt. M. von Richthofen	Germany	80
Capt. R. P. Fonk	France	75
Major E. Mannock	Britain	73
Lt. Col. W. A. Bishop	Britain	72
Lt. E. Udet	Germany	62
Major R. Callishaw	Britain	60

Air aces and their victims.

SOURCE **C**

SOURCE **D**

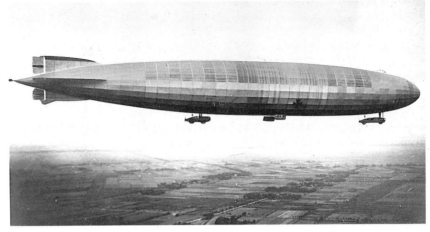

A Zeppelin.

SOURCE **F**

Artist's impression of First World War aircraft in combat.

SOURCE **E**

The Gotha bomber.

Barrage balloons with cable aprons.

Major changes came about through the use of **bomber aircraft**. From 1917 the Germans began using the Gotha IV bomber. It could carry a bomb load of 500 kilogrammes and was used to devastating effect. On 13 June twenty Gothas carried out a bombing raid on London in which 162 civilians were killed and 432 injured. One bomb fell on a school, killing 16 children and injuring 30 in an infant class. The British were horrified by the Gotha raids, which killed over 850 people. But it was not until 1918, when the Hanley Page Type 0/100 came into operation, that **reprisal raids** could be made. Then it was the turn of German civilians to experience the terror of the air raid. No-one would ever again doubt the value of the aeroplane in war.

EMPATHY

3.6 THE HOME FRONT

You read on pages 30–1 how in Britain the war was treated with great enthusiasm in 1914, but that the enthusiasm drained away as news of the horrific losses at the front reached home. Other factors also helped change people's attitude to the war. For the first time the British people were fighting a war which had far-reaching effects on their **everyday lives.**

This came as a shock to many people. Early in the war the government passed the **Defence of the Realm Act of 1914**. This gave the government wide powers to interfere in citizens' lives to a degree that had never been known before. DORA (as the Act became known) enabled the government to take over the running of the railways and mines, to censor newspapers and to control rents and prices. It also led to the start of British Summer Time, when the government ordered that clocks should be put forward an hour to give more daylight to work in. DORA was even used to cut down on pub opening hours and to water down beer. Less drunkenness meant more work, the government said.

The government also passed the **Military Service Acts of 1916**, calling up all men aged between 18 and 41 to join the army. This was called **conscription** (see page 42). With so many men away, there was a shortage of workers on the land and in the factories. **Women** stepped in to fill the vacancies. By 1918 millions of women were in full-time employment for the first time (pages 40–1).

In 1914 much of Britain's **food** came from abroad, especially from the Empire. Since the German submarines were sinking British merchant ships, a food shortage developed. In July 1918 **food rationing** was introduced. Well-off people, however, could usually obtain extra food if necessary on the **black market** – where food was sold illegally at higher prices. But conditions in Britain were nowhere near as bad as those in Germany, where there was a flourishing trade in potato peelings and there were food riots in the winter of 1916. Civilians also found their lives at risk in the war. The German Zeppelins and Gotha bombers carried out raids on Britain which killed nearly 1,400 people and injured over 3,300 more.

SOURCE A

'Bye, Son!' A soldier leaves for the war.

SOURCE B

'The whole street seemed to explode. There was smoke and flames all over, but the worst of all were the screams of the wounded and dying and mothers looking frantically for their kids.'

Account of a Zeppelin raid on Folkestone, 1917.

SOURCE C

'I can remember my mother going pale one afternoon as she saw the telegram boy coming towards the house. She turned to me and smiled as he cycled past, but she didn't say a word. My father and brother were in the navy, and you never knew if the telegram was for you.'

Memories of a girl aged 14 at the outbreak of war.

EMPATHY

Added to the risk of death or injury was the dreaded sight of the telegraph boy. These boys usually had the task of delivering the news that sons or husbands had been killed at the front (see page 52). The **death of a loved one** soon made people realize that there was nothing glorious about war. It also turned them against Germans living in Britain. It was not uncommon for German shopkeepers to have their premises stoned or looted after an air raid, and some Germans adopted English surnames. Even King George V, who was of German descent, changed his name to Windsor in 1917.

SOURCE D

Sometimes shops ran out of food.

SOURCE E

Looters attack a German-owned shop in London, June 1915.

EXERCISE

1 Study Source A.
 a How do you think the soldier going to war would have felt?
 b How might his mother have felt?
 c Would it have made any difference to your answer if you were told in which year the picture was taken?

2 Do you think that people would have supported the government when it took extra powers in 1914 (as in DORA)? Explain your answer.

3 Why did women in their millions take on the jobs left by men fighting at the front?

4 Read Source B.
 a Is it true to say that all Britons lived in constant fear of bombing attacks?
 b Why did some Britons suffer more from bombing attacks than others?

5 Look at Source D.
 a Is it true to say that all Britons suffered as a result of food shortages?
 b Why did some people suffer more than others from food shortages?

6 Read Source C.
 a Why did the girl's mother go pale?

 b Why do you think she 'smiled…but she didn't say a word'?

7 'It was not uncommon for German shopkeepers to have their premises stoned or looted after an air raid.'
 a Does this mean that German-owned shops wouldn't have been attacked if there had been no air raids?
 b Why else might people have attacked German-owned shops?
 c Did King George V change his name because he was frightened that Buckingham Palace would be attacked?

3.7 WOMEN AND THE WAR

CHANGE

The First World War caused a major change in the **position of women** in society and in **women's attitudes** to themselves. In 1914 women were still generally regarded by many men as second-class citizens. They were not even allowed to vote in general elections, let alone stand for Parliament or become Prime Minister.

Some women, the **Suffragettes**, had begun a campaign of violence and civil disobedience to bring their demands for political equality with men to the public's attention. Their behaviour had a twofold effect. Some people agreed that it was wrong that women could not vote; others said that by their irresponsible behaviour they were showing that women did not deserve the vote.

When the war broke out in 1914 the Suffragettes gave up their campaign and pledged their full support in the war effort. Impressed by the contribution made by women during the war, many men were forced to change their views. In 1918 women gained the vote, though they had to be aged 30 or more. Men could vote at the age of 21.

SOURCE A

Women chemical workers, Manchester 1918.

SOURCE B

Percentage of women to men in employment in Britain, 1914–20	Industry %	Transport %	Agriculture %	Commerce and finance %	All employment %
July 1914	26	2	9	27	24
July 1918	35	12	14	53	37
July 1920	27	4	10	40	28

SOURCE C

'That men must fight and women must weep is an old story now being told again.'

'The Lady' magazine, August 1914.

SOURCE D

'The war revolutionized the industrial position of women. It not only opened to them opportunities of employment but, more important even than this, it revolutionized men's minds and their conception of the sort of work which the ordinary everyday woman could do. It also opened their eyes to the national waste in condemning women to forms of work needing only very limited intelligence.'

M. Fawcett, 'The Women's Victory – and After', 1920.

SOURCE E

'During the war men and women were so thrown into daily contact that ideas about the sexes changed. Chaperons disappeared, and so did the delicate ignorance in which upper-class girls were kept. Many girls used language that would have shocked their mothers; many started to wear cosmetics, smoking became widespread and women bought drinks in public houses. Young girls were gripped by "khaki fever". By the end of the war the illegitimacy rate had increased by thirty per cent.'

Louise Black, in A. J. P. Taylor, 'The Twentieth Century', 1979.

SOURCE

Women training in a munitions factory, London, 1916.

SOURCE

'Many men realized for the first time that women could play a vital part in the nation's life and that they should be partners with men outside the home as well as inside. It became very difficult to believe the old arguments against votes for women, that they could not defend their country, that they did not understand politics, that they had fewer brains than men and so on.'

Comment on men's attitude to women in 1918 from L.E. Snellgrove, 'Suffragettes and Votes for Women', 1964.

EXERCISE

1 In what ways does Millicent Fawcett (Source D) believe that the position of women changed during the war?

2 Source B shows that an increased percentage of jobs were done by women during the war, but that the percentage of jobs done by women dropped again after the war.
  a Can you suggest any reason why the percentage dropped in the period 1918–20?
  b Does this mean that the position of working women didn't really change in the period 1914–20?

3 a What changes does Source E suggest took place during the war?

  b Do you think these changes were likely to be reversed after the war? Explain your answer.

4 Study Sources A, C, E and F.
  a How do these sources suggest the role of women changed?
  b Do these sources help you to decide whether the changes were real changes in attitudes, which were likely to be long-term rather than short-term? Give reasons for your answer.

5 Does the fact that women gained the vote in 1918 prove that there had been an improvement in their position? Explain your answer.

3.8 # VOLUNTEER OR CONSCRIPT?

 CAUSATION

We saw on pages 30–1 how in 1914 men volunteered willingly to fight in the war. In 1916 however Britain was forced to introduce **conscription** (compulsory military service). At first only single men were called up, but later on married men were conscripted as well. Since many men were undertaking jobs so important that they could not be spared, they were exempted from service. **Tribunals** were set up to hear appeals from men who had been called up but believed they fell into this category. Such men ranged from engine drivers and miners to those who were needed to plough the fields.

The tribunals also listened to the claims of **conscientious objectors** – men who said that their beliefs prevented them from taking part in war or from being involved in the killing of other humans. For many of Britain's 16,000 conscientious objectors the solution was to act as stretcher bearers, ambulancemen and so on. Yet 1,500 '**absolutists**' refused to have anything at all to do with the war, and more than 6,000 conscientious objectors were imprisoned at least once during the war.

SOURCE A

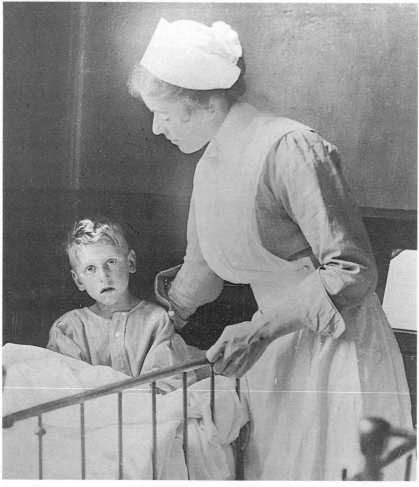

A child in hospital after being injured in an air raid.

SOURCE B

'So home I went each evening, with my rifle on my shoulder. As I walked through the streets people looked admiringly at me, and I felt more than ever pleased with myself. Girls smiled at me, men looked at me with respect, the bus drivers wished me luck and refused to take money for my fare, and everybody made way for me, as being on the King's business.'

British soldier commenting on his feelings after joining up.

SOURCE C

'In 1915 volunteers continued to come forward at the rate of 100,000 a month, urged on by a variety of reasons: hatred of the "Hun", a sense of duty, horror at German atrocities in Belgium, love of adventure, unemployment, and social pressure from friends, family, wives, sweethearts and neighbours.'

R. Huggett, 'The First World War', 1985.

SOURCE D

CAUSATION

SOURCE E

'The conscientious objector seemed to most people to be merely a shirker. The women he knew cut his acquaintance. His mother and brothers often jeered at him at home. He was chosen by his employer to be dispensed with. "Shirker", "coward", "dog", were the words they were thought to deserve.'

The Quaker leader John Graham explains the difficulties faced by a conscientious objector in the war.

SOURCE G

East-End women confront a non-volunteer with the white feather. (The white feather was given to men who were considered to be cowards.)

SOURCE F

'Thousands of conscientious objectors did heroic work that did not involve fighting. Many Quakers served as ambulancemen in the front lines and won medals for their bravery there.'

J. Brooman, 'The Great War', 1985.

SOURCE H

'The philosopher and mathematician Bertrand Russell was fined for issuing a pamphlet protesting at a two-year prison sentence imposed on a conscientious objector, deprived of his Cambridge lectureship, refused a passport to the United States where he had been offered a post at Harvard University, and in 1918 sentenced to six months' imprisonment for publishing a pacifist article.

J. Williams, 'The Home Fronts', 1972.

EXERCISE

1 a What made men join the army at the beginning of the war?
  b How many of these reasons would a conscientious objector accept as good reasons for helping the war effort?
  c Why did many of the conscientious objectors go to France to help in the war?

2 a Some men were granted exemption because they held such jobs as brewers. Does this suggest that the government was desperate for men to fight at the front?
  b Since there were only 16,000 conscientious objectors and most of them made some contribution to the war, why do you think the government was so keen to imprison those who would not help?

◀ *Conscientious objectors serving sentences of hard labour at a Scottish quarry.*

4.1 THE EASTERN FRONT, 1916–17

By the end of 1915 the **Russian army** had retreated over three hundred miles, and more than 10 million peasants had lost their homes. These people fled with the army and were forced to endure the hardships of the Russian winter with little food or shelter. Many of them froze to death.

During 1915 the Allies had tried to help the Russians by attacking Turkey at **Gallipoli** (see pages 26–7), but the campaign had ended in failure. In 1916 there seemed little more that they could do to improve Russia's terrible position. The Russians, however, were making a tremendous effort to help themselves. Their major problem in the first two years of the war had been lack of equipment. Now **Russian industry** was working all out to provide the supplies needed by the army (see Sources A and D). By the end of January 1916 Russia had a front-line strength of almost two million men, and virtually all of them had rifles. They were also well supplied with aircraft, telephones, gas masks, barbed wire and other essential war munitions.

Yet they were still lacking good generals. **Tsar Nicholas II** was so concerned at Russia's poor showing that he appointed himself commander-in-chief and sacked Grand Duke Nicholas, one of Russia's few talented generals. In February 1916 the Tsar ordered an attack on the Germans which was a dismal failure. Russia's casualties were enormous (see Source B). The Tsar had ordered the attack, and the Russian people blamed him for the defeat. They also blamed him for the terrible shortages they faced. By 1916 more than a third of Russian men were in the army. Many more were working in factories producing war goods. Not surprisingly, food production fell, and there was widespread hunger.

It was not all defeat for the Russians, however. In the south General Brusilov showed just what could be achieved when well-supplied men were led by generals with ability. In June 1916 the **Brusilov offensive** drove deep into Austria. By September the defending Austrians had lost over 600,000 men, and the Russians had advanced distances of up to seventy miles. The attack encouraged **Romania** to join the war on the Allies' side. But Brusilov's troops were exhausted. When the Germans diverted troops from the Western Front to help Austria, the Russians were forced to retreat. The Germans also defeated the Romanians with ease.

By the end of 1917 the Russian people had had enough of the war. Russia had not been defeated, but over two million of its soldiers had been killed, and millions more Russian peasants had died from the effects of the fighting. The Tsar had proved an incompetent general, and his government seemed to care little for the welfare of the people. In fact, since Tsar Nicholas had been at the front, the country had been virtually ruled by the sinister monk named **Rasputin**, who seemed to have some magical hold over the Tsar's wife, Alexandra.

SOURCE A

Percentage increase in Russian war production, 1914–17

Shells	2,000%
Rifles	1,100%
Guns	1,000%

SOURCE B

'No one knows the figures of Russian losses. Five or eight millions? No one knows the figures. All we know is that sometimes in our battles with the Russians we had to remove mounds of enemy corpses before our trench in order to get a clear field of fire against fresh assaulting waves.'

General Hindenburg commenting on Russian losses in the Tsar's offensive of February 1916.

SOURCE C

A Russian soldier tries to prevent his colleagues deserting. ▶

SOURCE **D**

Shell production in Russia, 1915–16

January 1915	358,000
November 1915	1,512,000
September 1916	2,900,000

SOURCE **E**

'Legend has a picture of countless millions of peasant soldiers being thrust into battle, armed with long-handled axes, against overpowering artillery and machine guns. It is a legend that owes nothing to reality.'

A historian's comment on the Russian army's standard of equipment in 1916.

The winter of 1916 was an unusually severe one. The people's discontent grew even more. That December, Rasputin was murdered, and in February 1917 there were widespread strikes and riots in Russia. In March the Tsar was forced to abdicate and was replaced by a new **Provisional Government**. This government wanted to continue the war and launched an attack on the Germans in July. After an early advance the Russians were soon in retreat once more. This was the last straw for many of the soldiers, who began to desert in huge numbers. Russia could no longer continue the war once so many of its troops had walked away from the front (see Source C).

The Russian people now turned against the Provisional Government and gave their support to **Lenin** and the **Bolsheviks**. Lenin promised '**peace, bread and land**' for the peasants. In November the Bolsheviks gained control of Russia and quickly signed an armistice with Germany. By the **Treaty of Brest-Litovsk** in March 1918 Russia granted Germany a huge slice of her land in return for peace. The war on the Eastern Front was over at last.

SOURCE **F**

Nicholas II, the last Tsar of Russia, in 1917.

4.2 THE UNITED STATES ENTERS THE WAR

CHANGE

In 1914, when war broke out in Europe, the **United States** chose to remain neutral. The 1916 US Presidential election was won by the Democrats with a slogan which talked of how President Wilson had 'kept us out of the war.' By 1918, however, US troops were operating with distinction on the Western Front, and by the end of the war over 100,000 Americans had lost their lives in fighting the Germans. Had the USA suddenly changed its mind about its role in international affairs?

SOURCE A

'Look abroad upon the troubled world. Only America at peace! Among all great powers of the world, only America saving her power for her own people. Do you not think it likely that the world will some time turn to America and say: "You were right and we were wrong?"'

US President Wilson, 1914.

SOURCE B

'It was on American industry that Great Britain especially depended for shells and other munitions during 1915 and 1916, while Great Britain was still painfully creating its chemical and munitions industries. Even in 1915 a third of all shells issued to the British army were made in North America.'

A. J. P. Taylor 'The Twentieth Century', 1979.

SOURCE C

United States loans to the Allies, 1914–18

Great Britain	$4,316 million
France	$2,852 million
Italy	£1,591 million
Russia	$341 million

SOURCE D

Cartoon of 1917 showing a British view of the USA's neutrality. ▼

SOURCE E

US cartoon of 1916 showing the German Ambassador as the Messenger of Death. ▼

SOURCE F

'Of primary significance among the reasons for the entry of the United States into the war is the fact that in general, from the start, American sympathies were predominantly with the Allies, and ultimately German provocation tipped the balance. Relations were not cordial with Germany, a nation regarded with suspicion as militaristic and unfriendly to democracy.'

T. H. Johnson, 'Oxford Companion to American History', 1966.

SOURCE G

'In January 1917 Zimmermann, Germany's Foreign Minister, sent a telegram to the German Ambassador in Mexico, directing him to seek an alliance. In return for Mexican co-operation, the Ambassador was to promise that Texas and other United States territory would be ceded to Mexico (after Germany's victory). The British, having deciphered the telegram, informed the United States of its contents.'

J. and G. Stokes, 'Europe and the Modern World, 1870–1970', 1973.

SOURCE H

US soldiers on the Western Front, 1918.

SOURCE I

'Over there, over there,
Send the word, send the word over there,
That the Yanks are coming, the Yanks are coming,
The drums rum-tumming everywhere.
So prepare, say a prayer,
Send the word, send the word to beware.
We'll be over, we're coming over,
And we won't come back till its over, over there.'

'George M. Cohen, 'Over There', 1917.

EXERCISE

1 President Wilson claimed that the 'world will some time turn to America and say: "You were right."'
   a What was the United States doing that was 'right'?
   b Why did Wilson think that neutrality was such a good idea?

2 Do you think that the German policy of sinking international ships that carried American passengers, and the attempt by the Germans to get the Mexicans on their side, were the cause of the USA's entry in to the war?

3 Source I shows an American's feelings when his country entered the war in 1917. In what way is his attitude similar to that shown in Source A?

4 'The policy of the United States never really changed during the period 1914–18.' Using the information in this unit, explain whether you agree or disagree with this statement.

4.3 THE WESTERN FRONT, 1917–18

In 1917 the United States joined the side of the Allies. But **General Nivelle**, the new French commander-in-chief, planned to bring about victory even before the USA's entry into the war. He was confident that if a breakthrough could be made in the west the German army could be quickly defeated.

Nivelle planned an attack using 5,000 artillery guns and over a million men, but there were faults with his plan. The attack was to be launched in an area where French forces had to cross steep and open ground to attack the German trenches. More importantly, the attack was expected by the Germans, and they had made plans to limit its effectiveness. During February and March 1917 they retreated to a new line of trenches called the **Hindenburg Line**. They destroyed the villages they had evacuated and laid booby-traps for advancing soldiers. Even the French government began to have doubts about the attack. Yet Nivelle was so confident and his men were so keen for victory that the attack went ahead.

On 9 April the British attacked the Germans at **Arras**. This move was designed to divert German troops away from the area of the French attack. North of Arras at Vimy Ridge the **Canadians** scored a spectacular victory, capturing 4,000 Germans, though at great cost to their own army. When the attack was called off a week later, the British troops had gained six miles of land and had captured 14,000 Germans. But British casualties were over 100,000.

On 16 April, Nivelle launched his great offensive. It was a terrible failure. German machine guns took a heavy toll of French troops, who Nivelle had expected to advance six miles on the first day. They managed six hundred yards. The French government reminded Nivelle of his promise to call off the attack if no breakthrough was made in the first two days. Yet he persisted. After two weeks the French casualties stood at close to 200,000. It was too much for soldiers who had been promised glorious victory. Across the front there was an outbreak of mutinies. Men refused to fight and turned for home (see pages 30–1). At one stage almost half the French army was refusing to obey orders.

In desperation the French government sacked Nivelle and appointed the hero of Verdun (see pages 20–1), **General Pétain**, to take command. Pétain restored order by court-martialling thousands of the mutineers and by improving the fighting and living conditions of the other soldiers. Fortunately for the French, the Germans were unaware of the seriousness of the mutinies and did not attack. France's allies were told only that no more could be expected from the French in 1917.

In July 1917 the British launched a major attack at **Passchendaele**. Conditions were appalling. Officers could hardly believe that the men were expected to fight in mud which came up to their waists. Once again an artillery bombardment was followed by an infantry advance. Once again casualties were horrific, and very little was gained. By November the British had advanced eight hundred yards and had lost 250,000 men. The German casualties were nearer 300,000.

SOURCE A

Canadian machine gunners entrenched in a shell hole during the battle of Passchendaele, 1917.

SOURCE B

'This is it, mates! If we don't get 'em this time, we'll never get 'em! What a thrashing they are going to get! There are guns all over the place – and big ones at that! The men are already drunk with victory.'

French soldier before Nivelle's offensive.

SOURCE C

'The battlefield was turned into one huge quagmire, into which were sucked men, horses, guns, it being impossible to extricate them, when once they were in the grip of this terrible mud.'

Second Lieutenant James Dale, Liverpool Scottish Regiment, describing Passchendaele.

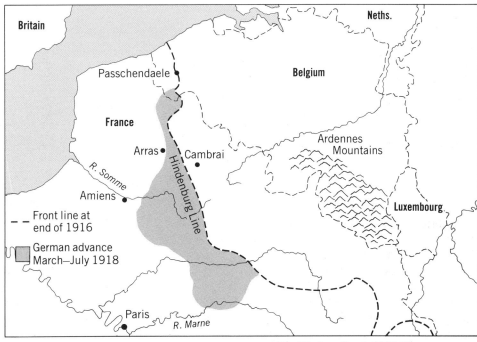

The Western Front, 1917–18.

The methods of attack used were resulting in enormous slaughter. Then, in November, church bells in London rang out to celebrate a British victory brought about by new tactics. At **Cambrai**, British tanks (see pages 50–1) drove deep into the enemy lines. Yet the victory was short-lived. The infantry could not keep up with the tanks, and a German counter-offensive soon regained the captured land. The German generals knew that time was not on their side, however. Not only were the German people running short of food, but when the first United States soldiers arrived on the Western Front a German victory would be almost impossible. Therefore it was decided in Germany to make one dramatic all-out attempt to win victory on the Western Front. Since Russia had left the war, Germany had transfered almost half a million men from the east. The time had come to use them.

On 21 March 1918 **General Ludendorff** launched **Operation Michael**. Ludendorff planned to drive through the weakest part of the Allied lines and to bypass strongpoints. An artillery bombardment, followed by clouds of mustard gas, marked the opening of the campaign. At first it was brilliantly successful. The British retreated in disarray as the German advance took them beyond the river Somme and eventually to the banks of the river Marne. Once again Paris was under threat. But Ludendorff's army was short of supplies and had advanced too quickly for the supplies to keep up. On 8 August the Allies, now reinforced with fresh US troops, halted the advance. Ludendorff talked of 'the black day of the German Army', and from then on the Allies pushed the Germans back. Three days later Ludendorff, realizing that his gamble had failed, informed the Kaiser: 'We have nearly reached the limit of our powers of resistance. The war must be ended.'

SOURCE D

THE SANDS RUN OUT.

The Kaiser sees time running out for his armies, 1918 cartoon.

ACTIVITY

Make a time-line to show the main events on the Western Front in 1917 and 1918.

CHANGE

4.4 ENTER THE TANK

SOURCE A

The Mark I tank, 1916.

SOURCE B

'The virtue of tanks was that they could cross trenches, break through barbed wire, force their way over shell-pocked ground and deal with machine guns. They were there to aid the infantry to do what modern conditions of war were making it increasingly difficult to do.'

M. Brown, 'Tommy Goes to War.' 1972.

SOURCE C

'The Mark IV was not all that much in advance of the Mark I. Its new bullet-proof armour turned out to be no such thing against the German armour-piercing bullets. It had the same engine, the same armament, the same crew, the same speed; it was unhandy to drive and control, and interior temperatures often rose to 120 degrees. It was, in other words, no war winner.'

J. Terraine, 'White Heat: The New Warfare, 1914–18', 1982.

SOURCE D

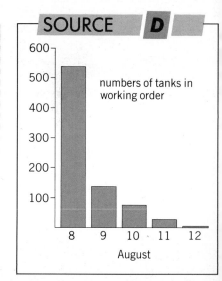

Number of tanks in working order at the Battle of Amiens, 8–12 August 1918.

SOURCE E

'The pulses of one crew were taken immediately they got out of their tank; the beats averaged 130 to the minute or just twice as fast as they should have been. Two men of one crew lost their reason and had to be restrained by force, and one tank commander became delirious. In some cases where infantry were carried in the tank, they fainted within three-quarters of an hour of the start.'

An officer's account of the effect of being inside tanks in battle.

SOURCE G

'Their effect was largely moral. They did a good service in crushing machine-gun posts and in village fighting. The infantry liked to see them, and as the enemy has invariably exaggerated the numbers employed, and has often reported their presence when there was none, he evidently stood in fear of them.'

Brigadier-General Sir J. E. Edmonds (a British Commander), 1918.

SOURCE H

'Because armoured warfare became a developing theme in the post-war years and a very important element in the Second World War, tanks have been singled out as the decisive weapon of 1918. This is mythology. They bore about as much relation to the tanks of the Second World War as a 1908 Model-T Ford does to a Jaguar.'

J. Terraine, 'White Heat: The New Warfare, 1914–18', 1982.

SOURCE F

British tank abandoned on the battlefield.

EXERCISE

1 Using the sources in this unit, together with your knowledge of the First World War, explain whether you agree or disagree with each of the following statements. Explain your answer.
   a 'When they were first introduced in 1916, tanks were so unreliable that they were of little value to the army.'
   b 'The design of tanks so improved that they brought about a major change in the way that war was fought.'
   c 'By the end of 1918 tanks had become the most decisive weapon used.'

2 Do you agree that, if tanks could not be made to work properly, then the army was wasting its time trying to use them?

4.5 ONE IN FIVE

EMPATHY

Casualties in the First World War were appallingly high. Twenty million soldiers were wounded, and over eight million were killed. In the British army one in five of the soldiers never came home. The casualties meant immense sadness not only for those who witnessed the horror of war, but also for those at home who lived in hope of the safe return of their loved ones.

SOURCE A

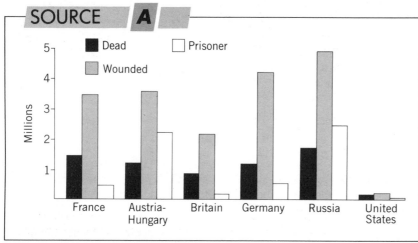

Losses in the war.

SOURCE B

A British soldier pays his respects to a fallen mate.

SOURCE C

'The chances for any front line soldier were not good. Out of nearly 5 million men who joined the British Army between 1914 and 1918, one in every five was killed and two out of the remaining four were wounded.'

T. Howarth, 'The Western Front', 1976

SOURCE D

'I have been requested to convey to you and to your family an expression of the utmost sympathy with you on the death of your husband… . Your husband died quite instantaneously, while on duty, as the result of a shell bursting in the trench. I must say that his injuries were mostly internal and caused no disfigurement of the features… .'

Letter from the platoon sergeant to a soldier's widow.

SOURCE E

'One of the casualties was an oldish man, and the distorted lump where his body should have been gave a horrifying effect: a wooden wedge was held fiercely between his teeth and his eyes flashed around with an extraordinary speed, implying such frantic agony that I had to look away.'

The reality of death at the Somme, 1916. From M.Brown 'Tommy Goes to War', 1978.

SOURCE F

Two of the 20 million men wounded in the war.

SOURCE G

'Does it matter – losing your legs?
For people will always be kind,
And you need not show that you mind
When others come in after hunting
to gobble their muffins and eggs.

Does it matter – losing your sight?…
There's so much splendid work for the blind;
And people will always be kind,
As you sit on the terrace remembering
And turning your face to the light.

Do they matter – those dreams from the pit?…
You can drink and forget and be glad,
And people won't say that you're mad;
For they'll know that you've fought for your country
And no one will worry a bit.'

◀ *Poem by Siegfried Sassoon, 1917.*

SOURCE H

'I had two brothers in the war. One was killed in the Dardanelles. He was reported missing. We never knew what happened to him. The other one was reported missing in France.'

From R. Huggett, 'The First World War', 1985.

EXERCISE

1 In Source D the widow is informed that her husband died 'instantaneously' and that there was no 'disfigurement' of his body.
   a How would the widow have felt when she received this news?
   b It was much more likely that the soldier died a death similar to that of the man in Source E. Why, then would the sergeant lie to the widow?

2 Many relatives have travelled to the graves of dead soldiers since the war.
   a Why do you think they have done so?
   b Is there any reason why the brother of the men killed in Source H should feel even greater grief than relatives of other men killed?

3 'Men who were wounded in the service of their country felt no bitterness, just pride.' Do you think that this statement is likely to be correct? Give reasons for your answer.

4.6 THE WAR IN OTHER PARTS OF THE WORLD

Although the First World War is best known for fighting on the Western and Eastern Fronts, it was fought over a much larger area. In **Europe** there was fighting in both Italy and Greece, and when Turkey entered the war the conflict spread to the deserts of the **Middle East**. German colonies came under attack in **Africa**, and there were also clashes in the islands of the **Pacific**. This truly was a *world* war.

Before the outbreak of war **Italy** had been part of the **Triple Alliance** with Germany and Austria-Hungary (see page 6). Yet Italy did not enter the war in 1914. In 1916 when the Italians eventually joined in, it was on the side of the Allies. Italy hoped that Austria-Hungary would lose the war and that there would be gains to be made on Austria's border. In a campaign fought high in the Alps, however, the Italian offensives against Austria went badly. They were held up at the river Isonzo and only after eleven battles were they able to cross it. Their success was short-lived as the Germans rushed in reinforcements and inflicted a major defeat on the Italians at **Caporetto**. But with British and French help the Italians recovered, and in September 1918 they scored a dramatic victory over the Austrians at **Vittorio Veneto**.

The British campaign against the Turks at **Gallipoli** (see page 26) had been a dismal failure. An equally unsuccessful attempt was made to form a front in **Greece**. The Allies tried to help **Serbia** by landing troops in Greece. But they could not persuade the Greeks to join the war. Nearly half a million British and French troops spent the war in Greece, fighting very little.

There was more success for the Allies in the Arabian deserts of the Middle East. One of Britain's major fears in this area was that it might lose control of the **Suez Canal**, which was an important route to India and the Far East. From 1915 British and Indian

Austrian forces on the attack in the snows of the Alps.

Map 1: The war around the world.

SOURCE **B**

Lawrence of Arabia.

troops fought the **Turks** in Mesopotamia, but in April 1916 they suffered a heavy defeat at **Kut**. This was their only major set-back, however, and by the end of the war they had won control of the whole of Mesopotamia.

One factor in the British success was the work of **Colonel T. E. Lawrence**. He was sent by the British to give support to the **Arabs** who were rebelling against their Turkish rulers. 'Lawrence of Arabia', as he soon became known, helped the Arabs to fight an effective campaign of guerrilla warfare against the Turks. The most significant success was brought about by **General Allenby**, commander of the British forces guarding the Suez Canal. He was able to take advantage of Lawrence's work to launch attacks on the Turks in **Palestine**. In December 1917 Allenby captured Jerusalem, and in September 1918 he launched his final offensive. In quick succession he captured Damascus, Beirut and Allepo. On 30 October the Turks accepted defeat and signed an armistice ending their part in the war.

Further success for the Allies came in Africa. Germany held four colonies here; three of them – Togoland, the Cameroons and German South-West Africa – were captured by 1916. Only German East Africa held out and did not surrender until the end of the war.

Germany was to lose its other colonies too. **Japan** took the base of Kiaochow in China and the Marshall, Caroline and Marianne Islands in the Pacific. The remaining German Pacific possessions, Samoa and New Guinea, were captured by Anzac forces. By 1918 Germany no longer had an empire. Its defeat in Europe had been matched by defeats all around the world.

Map 2: The Italian campaign.

Map 3: The campaign in the Middle East.

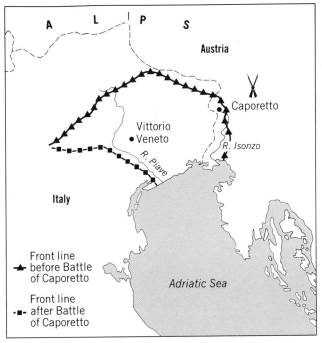

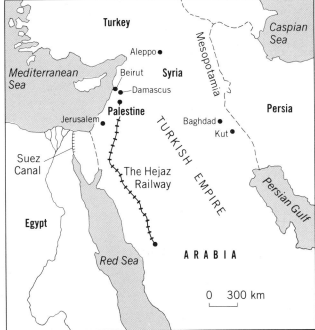

5.1 THE END OF THE WAR

By August 1918 **Ludendorff's** gamble in attacking the Allies had failed (see page 49). On 8 August ('the black day of the German Army') the counter-attack began. Taking advantage of their tank superiority the Allies pushed forward until they had broken through the **Hindenburg Line**. The Germans put up brave resistance, but their spirit was broken, and they suffered enormous casualties in the last months of the war. Realizing that defeat was inevitable, on 3 October the German Chancellor, **Prince Max of Baden**, asked the United States to arrange an end to the fighting. Matters were made worse for the Germans by the collapse of their allies. **Bulgaria** made peace on 29 September, followed by **Turkey** one month later. Finally **Austria** suffered defeat at the hands of the Italians at Vittorio Veneto and signed an armistice with the Allies on 4 November.

The effects of four years of fighting proved too much for the German people. They had had enough of war and the hardship it caused. As an outbreak of **influenza** swept through the country (on one day alone 1,722 Berliners died in the epidemic), **riots** flared up. There were even fears for the Kaiser's safety. On 29 October the navy mutinied at **Kiel**, and this was followed by widespread uprisings. First Munich and then Berlin fell into the hands of revolutionaries. In a bid to restore order Prince Max persuaded the Kaiser to abdicate, and on 9 November he fled to Holland. Two days later, in a railway carriage in the French forest of **Compiègne**, the Germans agreed to the Allies' terms for an **armistice**. It was all over.

SOURCE A

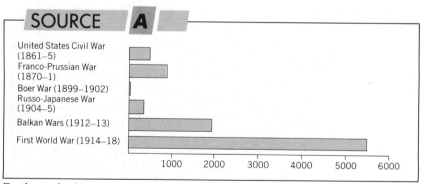

United States Civil War (1861–5)	
Franco-Prussian War (1870–1)	
Boer War (1899–1902)	
Russo-Japanese War (1904–5)	
Balkan Wars (1912–13)	
First World War (1914–18)	

1000 2000 3000 4000 5000 6000

Deaths per day in major wars.

SOURCE B

Communist revolutionaries armed in Berlin, 1918. ▼

SOURCE C

British soldiers in the summer of 1918 sporting their 'trophies'.

SOURCE D

Victims of the war; the dead, placed under wooden crosses, await burial.

SOURCE E

'All the mill sirens went off. We were in school and we were called up to the Assembly Hall and sang, "Rule Britannia". Then we were sent home. Someone gave me 6d (2½p), and I bought a flag. Everyone celebrated outside the Town Hall, and we all sang "God Save the King."'

Memories of Armistice Day, Rose Greaves, aged 10 in 1918.

SOURCE F

Celebration in London, November 1918.

SOURCE G

Celebrations in France, November 1918 – a soldier returns to his wife.

CAUSATION

5.2 WAS GERMANY STARVED INTO SUBMISSION?

SOURCE A

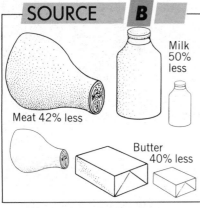

Berlin, 1917: flowerbeds are turned into allotments to provide badly needed food.

During the First World War the British and the Germans tried to prevent supplies reaching each other. The British used their **naval superiority** to blockade German ports, while the Germans used **submarines** to sink Allied merchant shipping in the Atlantic. By 1917 the citizens of both countries found themselves short of food. The British managed to defeat the submarine threat (see page 33), but the Germans were never able to lift the British blockade. By 1918 the German people were starving. Some historians believe that it was this **starvation** which caused the Germans to sue for peace.

SOURCE B

Milk 50% less

Meat 42% less

Butter 40% less

Decrease in German food production, 1914–18.

SOURCE C

'Poor German production figures – 30 to 40 per cent less than before the war in 1917 – revealed not so much inefficient leadership as the weariness of an underfed people.'

A. J. P. Taylor, 'The Twentieth Century', 1979.

SOURCE D

'By 1918 Ludendorff was growing short of the means of waging war – essential supplies of rubber, oil and fodder. The great German war machine was giving way under the constant strain of 3½ years of fighting. Germany could not go on much longer.'

B. Catchpole, 'A Map History of the Modern World', 1968.

SOURCE E

'Once the Americans were in, the result was almost certain to be a German defeat. The United States had vast supplies of manpower and materials, far greater than the Germans could achieve. Germany fast became exhausted; so too did Britain and France – but they could be boosted by America. And yet the Germans attacked. This weakened them. The Allies could then strike back, greatly aided by newly arrived American support.'

M. Holden, 'War in the Trenches', 1973.

SOURCE F

'Wedged between his starving family and a hopeless future, the German soldier's morale was shattered by the realization that the succession of offensives since 21 March 1918 had been in vain.'

Major-General J. F. C. Fuller, 'The Decisive Battles of the Western World', 1955.

SOURCE G

Capturing army	Prisoners	Guns
British	188,700	2,840
French	139,000	1,880
United States	43,000	1,421
Belgian	14,500	474

German losses 18 July – 11 November 1918.

SOURCE H

'The conclusion is inescapable that Germany and her allies were defeated in the field.'

Prime Minister Lloyd George.

SOURCE ▌ *I* ▌

German prisoners of war, August 1918.

EXERCISE

1 Sources A and B show that Germany suffered a food shortage in the war. 'Britain also suffered a food shortage, yet Britain did not lose; therefore food shortage was not a cause of Germany's defeat.' Explain whether you agree or disagree with this statement.

2 What other reasons for Germany's defeat are given in Sources C and D? Can the food shortage be blamed for this?

3 The Germans knew that if Ludendorff's offensive failed they would quickly lose the war. Germany could have stayed on the defensive and dragged the war out. Then it could probably have negotiated better peace terms. Why then wasn't Ludendorff prevented from launching his attack?

4 In what way did the following contribute to Germany's defeat in the war?
  a The failure to defeat the British navy at Jutland (see page 32).
  b The defeat of Germany's allies (see pages 54–7).
  c The development of tanks by the British (see pages 50–1).

5 How important a factor is the shortage of food in considering why Germany lost the war?

5.3 HANG THE KAISER!

EMPATHY

In November 1918 the German government negotiated an **armistice** with the Allies. The war was over, and fighting stopped. However, there still remained the tricky issue of the **peace treaty**. The Allies faced the task of creating a treaty which would both satisfy their own people and maintain peace for years to come. This was difficult enough, but they also had to reach their decisions in an atmosphere of hatred towards the Germans. Many people, particularly the French, wanted revenge for what had happened. One British newspaper called on the Allies to 'Hang the Kaiser'. Just how widespread were such feelings?

SOURCE A

'Germany is going to pay, and I personally have no doubt that we will get everything out of her that you can squeeze out of a lemon and bit more. Not only all the gold Germany has got, but all her silver and jewels shall be handed over.'

Sir Eric Geddes, British MP, speaking in 1918.

SOURCE B

French losses in the war

Forest laid waste (sq. miles)	1,857
Farmland laid waste (sq. miles)	8,000
Houses destroyed	300,000
Factories destroyed	6,000
Schools destroyed	1,500
Churches destroyed	1,200
Livestock lost	1,300,000

SOURCE D

One of the many French cemeteries on the Western Front.

SOURCE C

The Belgian town of Ypres after the war.

SOURCE E

LOCAL HEROES
" The Work they did was A

Casualties incurred by the 16th West Yorkshire Battalion in the Somme offensive, August 1916.

SOURCE H

'The poor French people were pathetically grateful to us, and their tales of Hun brutality were horrible. For the first time we realised that the newspaper reports of brutality etc. were quite true and in fact very mildly written.'

British soldier describes the reaction of French villagers, October 1918.

EXERCISE

1 Sir Eric Geddes (Source A) talks of how Germany should be squeezed like a lemon.
   a Why would a British politician talk that way in 1918?
   b Woodrow Wilson was a United States politician. Why didn't he feel the same way towards the Germans as Sir Eric Geddes?

2 Who do you think the soldiers at the front were more likely to agree with, Geddes or Wilson? Explain your answer.

3 a How do you think French civilians living near the Western Front would have felt about what should happen to Germany after the war?
   b Do you think that their views would have been shared by the rest of France? Explain your answer.

4 'Britain wasn't invaded by Germany, and its civilians didn't experience acts of brutality by German soldiers. Therefore the British people didn't feel as bitter towards the Germans as the French did.' Explain whether you agree or disagree with this statement.

GREAT ADVANCE.

SOURCE F

'The Hun is a strange fellow. We are constantly gingering him up with raids and artillery shots. On the whole he fights very well against odds, and I can't help admiring him.'

Sapper Garfield Powell, Royal Engineers, 1916.

SOURCE G

'We are not enemies of the German people, and they are not our enemies.'

US President Woodrow Wilson speaking in 1919.

5.4 THE PARIS PEACE CONFERENCE

PEACE AND FUTURE CANNON FODDER

The Tiger: "Curious! I seem to hear a child weeping!"

Cartoon, 1919. The men shown are, from left to right, Lloyd George, Orlando the Italian leader, Clemenceau and Wilson.

In January 1919 representatives from over thirty nations gathered in **Paris** to decide the fate of the defeated nations (Germany, Austria-Hungary, Turkey and Bulgaria). In reality the talks were dominated by the '**Big Three**': United States President Woodrow Wilson, French Prime Minister Georges Clemenceau and British Prime Minister David Lloyd George. These men were to make the decisions. The defeated nations had no part in negotiating the terms, and because of its Communist government Russia was not welcome at the talks.

The 'Big Three' had different ideas about what should be done. **Clemenceau** wanted to make Germany pay for the damage it had caused in France, and to make it so weak that it could never again attack France. **Wilson**, on the other hand, saw no reason to punish Germany. He felt the war was not entirely Germany's fault, and now that the fighting had stopped it was time to create fair treaties which would keep peace in Europe. In 1918 Wilson had published his **Fourteen Points**, which he saw as a blueprint for peace. These included arms reduction and the setting up of a **League of Nations** to prevent future warfare. Now was the time to put his plans into operation. **Lloyd George** was in a difficult position; he thought that if Germany was treated too harshly it would want to fight a war of revenge in future years. If treated leniently, Germany could still be a valuable trading partner. But many of Lloyd George's fellow Britons saw the situation differently and wanted Germany punished (see pages 60–1).

In the event, Clemenceau and those seeking to punish Germany were to be happiest with the peace treaties.

Terms of the Treaty of Versailles
- A **League of Nations** was to be established.
- Germany was forced to give up its **colonies** in Africa and the Pacific (see pages 54–5). These were to be administered by the Allies under the control of the League of Nations. These **mandates**, as they were called, would eventually gain independence. The League also took Memel, Danzig and the Saar, with the Saar coalfields going to France for fifteen years.
- All the **land** that Germany had taken from Russia in 1918 was taken back, and Germany was divided by giving the new Poland access to the sea in West Prussia. Land was also lost in the north to Denmark, and in the west to Belgium and France.
- Germany was **forbidden to unite** with Austria (*Anschluss*). An area fifty kilometres wide on the east bank of the Rhine was to be **demilitarized**. Germany could not keep soldiers, weapons or fortifications in this area – although the Allies intended to station troops there for fifteen years.
- The German **army** was cut to 100,000 men and the **navy** limited to six battleships. Germany was not allowed to build tanks, planes or battleships.
- Germany had to agree to Article 231 – the war guilt clause – accepting **full blame** for starting the war. It would have to pay **reparations** to cover the cost of the damage. This sum was calculated in 1921 to be £6.6 million.

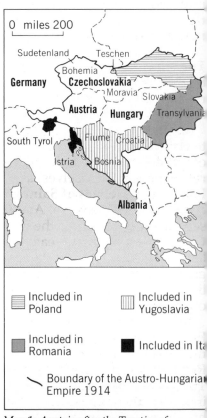

0 miles 200

Germany

Sudetenland
Bohemia
Czechoslovakia
Moravia
Slovakia
Austria Hungary Transylvania
South Tyrol
Fiume Croatia
Istria Bosnia

Teschen

Albania

Included in Poland

Included in Yugoslavia

Included in Romania

Included in Ita

Boundary of the Austro-Hungaria Empire 1914

Map 1: Austria after the Treaties of Saint Germain and Trianon.

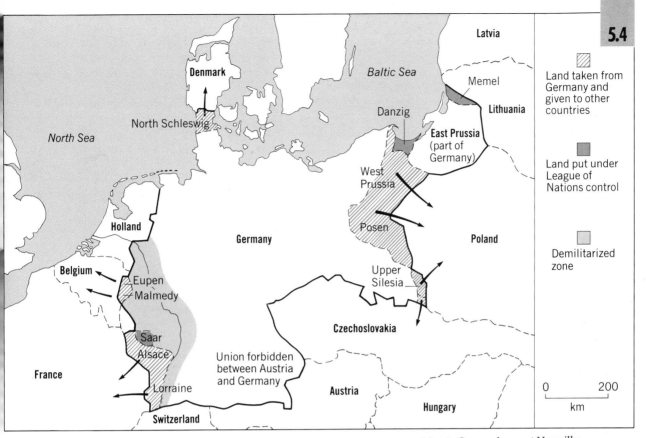

Map 2: German losses at Versailles.

Germany condemned the Treaty of Versailles as a diktat (an imposed settlement), and the German government resigned rather than agree to it. But there was no real choice, and the new government reluctantly accepted the terms.

The other treaties

By the **Treaty of Neuilly** (1919), **Bulgaria** had to pay reparations, reduce its armed forces and suffer land losses. Austria-Hungary and Turkey were to prove greater problems.

In 1918 the various peoples of **Austria-Hungary** had begun to claim their independence. This was in keeping with the idea of **self determination** (the right of people living under foreign rule to govern themselves) as set out in Wilson's Fourteen Points. The **Treaties of Saint Germain and Trianon** (1919) confirmed this break-up. Austria and Hungary became separate countries, and the new states of **Yugoslavia** and **Czechoslovakia** were created. Austria and Hungary also lost land to Italy and Poland. But the treaty-makers had failed to give full self determination; there were now 3 million Germans living in Czechoslovakia and 400,000 Slavs in Italy. This could only cause trouble in the future.

In the **Treaty of Sèvres** (1920), **Turkey** lost most of its European lands. Its empire in the Middle East was divided into mandates to be controlled by the French and the British. Reparations and cuts in the armed forces were also imposed. The Turks rebelled against these terms, which were improved in the **Treaty of Lausanne** (1923). Peace had been established, but the mistakes made in this period were to be a major cause of the renewed hostilities which broke out in 1939.

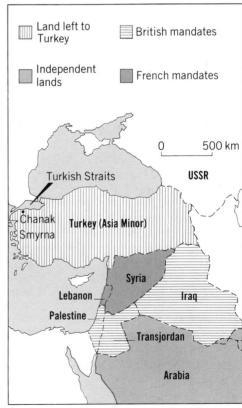

Map 3: The Turkish Empire after the Treaty of Sèvres.

INDEX